Anchorage

ALASKA GEOGRAPHIC / Volume 23, Number 1

To teach many more to better know and more wisely use our natural resources...

EDITOR
Penny Rennick

PRODUCTION DIRECTOR
Kathy Doogan

STAFF WRITER
L.J. Campbell

MARKETING MANAGER
Pattey Parker Mancini

BOARD OF DIRECTORS
Richard Carlson
Kathy Doogan
Penny Rennick

Robert A. Henning, **PRESIDENT EMERITUS**

POSTMASTER: Send address changes to:

***ALASKA GEOGRAPHIC*®**
P.O. Box 93370
Anchorage, Alaska 99509-3370

PRINTED IN U.S.A.

ISBN: 1-56661-030-3

Price to non-members this issue: $21.95

COVER: *The downtown Anchorage skyline overlooks Cook Inlet and the Chugach Mountains. (Danny Daniels)*

PREVIOUS PAGE: *Inner and outer Westchester Lagoon flank Minnesota Drive near the mouth of Chester Creek. (Alaskana Photo-Art)*

FACING PAGE: *A juggler performs at the Saturday Market, held each summer weekend in a parking lot off 3rd Avenue. (Richard Montagna)*

***ALASKA GEOGRAPHIC*®** (ISSN 0361-1353) is published quarterly by The Alaska Geographic Society, 639 West International Airport Road, Unit 38, Anchorage, AK 99518. Second-class postage paid at Anchorage, Alaska, and additional mailing offices. Copyright © 1996 by The Alaska Geographic Society. All rights reserved. Registered trademark: Alaska Geographic, ISSN 0361-1353; Key title Alaska Geographic.

THE ALASKA GEOGRAPHIC SOCIETY is a non-profit, educational organization dedicated to improving geographic understanding of Alaska and the North, putting geography back in the classroom and exploring new methods of teaching and learning.

MEMBERS RECEIVE *ALASKA GEOGRAPHIC*®, a high-quality quarterly publication that devotes each issue to monographic, in-depth coverage of a northern region or resource-oriented subject.

MEMBERSHIP in The Alaska Geographic Society costs $39 per year, $49 to non-U.S. addresses ($31.20 of the membership fee is for a one-year subscription to *ALASKA GEOGRAPHIC*®.) Back issues are also available. To order or request a free catalog of available back issues, contact: The Alaska Geographic Society, Box 93370, Anchorage, AK 99509-3370; phone (907) 562-0164, fax (907) 562-0479, e-mail: akgeo@anc.ak.net.

SUBMITTING PHOTOGRAPHS: Please write for a list of upcoming topics or other specific photo needs and a copy of our editorial guidelines. We cannot be responsible for unsolicited submissions. Submissions not accompanied by sufficient postage for return by certified mail will be returned by regular mail.

CHANGE OF ADDRESS: The post office does not automatically forward *ALASKA GEOGRAPHIC*® when you move. To ensure continuous service, please notify us at least six weeks before moving. Send your new address and membership number or a mailing label from a recent *ALASKA GEOGRAPHIC*® to: Alaska Geographic Society, Box 93370, Anchorage, AK 99509. If your book is returned to us by the post office, we will contact you to ask if you wish to receive a replacement for $5 (for postage charges).

COLOR SEPARATIONS: Graphic Chromatics

PRINTING: The Hart Press

The Library of Congress has cataloged this serial
publication as follows:

Alaska Geographic. v.1-
[Anchorage, Alaska Geographic Society] 1972-
v. ill. (part col.). 23 x 31 cm.
Quarterly
Official publication of The Alaska Geographic Society.
Key title: Alaska geographic, ISSN 0361-1353.

1. Alaska—Description and travel—1959-
—Periodicals. I. Alaska Geographic Society.

F901.A266   917.98'04'505   72-92087

Library of Congress 75[79112] MARC-S.

ABOUT THIS ISSUE: Anchorage is a big part of Alaska, and certainly the biggest part of urban Alaska. So it seems appropriate that *ALASKA GEOGRAPHIC*® take a closer look at northern North America's largest city. Those writing about Anchorage are fortunate that the city is so young, that some of those who built its history still travel its streets. A handful of the city's residents moved here when the town was born. They are Anchorage's living history, and to them this issue is dedicated.

We thank Charles Wohlforth for his article on pioneers Bill and Lilian Stolt, Scott Banks for telling readers about his experiences around Campbell Airstrip and the wilderness park in east Anchorage. And we thank Jill Shepherd for her vivid highlights of the gardens of Anchorage. *ALASKA GEOGRAPHIC*® staff, chiefly staff writer L.J. Campbell and to a lesser extent editor Penny Rennick, wrote the bulk of the text. They acknowledge the help of many residents, in particular James Fall, anthropologist with the Alaska Department of Fish and Game; Joan M. Antonson, Alaska state historian; Dan Fleming and Bruce Merrell of the Alaska Collection, Z.J. Loussac Library; Mina Jacobs, assistant librarian with the Anchorage Museum of History and Art; pioneers John Bagoy and Steve McCutcheon; Fred Brown of Shannon & Wilson Inc., Bill Butler and his staff with the state Department of Transportation; and Christine Miller, planner with the state Department of Community and Regional Affairs.

Contents

The Government's Child

When Andrew Christensen gathered the men to his platform on the mud flats of Ship Creek the afternoon of July 10, 1915, he formalized the birth of Anchorage, giving legitimacy and organization to what one Boston professor called "a bulging fantasy." Anchorage may not have been much more than a fantasy then, but in the ensuing 81 years, it has grown to be anything but a fantasy. This is the story of that frontier birth and its growth to urban adulthood.

In 1778, when Capt. James Cook sailed up what the British Earl of Sandwich labeled Cook's River, he anchored within site of a glacier-scoured lowland flanked by two arms of water and a range of mountains. Cook was looking for the Northwest Passage between the Pacific and Atlantic and wasted little time in sailing onward once he determined that this river didn't lead to the Atlantic. Before he left, however, he named the southern of the two arms "River Turnagain." Two of his crewmen who explored the area later recognized Cook's River as an inlet, and Capt. George Vancouver,

LEFT: *Downtown Anchorage still has remnants of its pioneer history, such as this log house, and the city has residents who arrived when the community was first established. At times these pioneers gather to share their memories, and each February the pioneers put on a pancake feed as part of Fur Rondy. The sourdough residents are part of the living history that is the hallmark of Anchorage and of Alaska. (Danny Daniels)*

FACING PAGE: *The hub of downtown Anchorage is the log cabin visitor center at 4th Avenue and F Street. Walking tours start here, and the center provides information on Anchorage and Southcentral Alaska destinations. The building behind the cabin is the Old City Hall, which is being restored as offices for the convention and visitors bureau. In summer, live music is performed on the green in front of the building. (Danny Daniels)*

Dena'ina Country

Long before the first white homesteaders, the land known today as Anchorage was home to Dena'ina (Tanaina) Athabaskan Indians.

The Dena'ina living in upper Cook Inlet may have numbered as many as 1,000 in the days before contact, out of a total precontact Dena'ina population of perhaps 5,000. The Dena'ina ranged as far west as Lake Iliamna, Lake Clark and upper Stony River, as far north as the Alaska Range, and as far south as the Kenai Peninsula. Several distinct groups of Dena'ina lived in upper Cook Inlet. These groups — the Knik Arm, Susitna River and Tyonek Dena'ina — were generally delineated by their winter village sites. The Knik Dena'ina, whose winter villages also included Eklutna, used the Anchorage region extensively for seasonal hunting and fishing.

Dena'ina elder Shem Pete, who grew up in the area and remembered seeing the tents of Anchorage for the first time in 1914, provided much of the information known about the upper Cook Inlet Dena'ina and traditional place names of the region. His stories were collected during a period of years before his death by linguist James Kari and anthropologist James Fall, among others. The book *Shem Pete's Alaska* (1987), compiled by Kari and Fall, contains many of his stories and descriptions of his people's home territory.

The Dena'ina may have moved into upper

Shown here with his wife and child, Chief Wassily represented the Knik Dena'ina, who depended on the Anchorage bowl for important subsistence resources. (Photo No. B82.52.273, Anchorage Museum)

Cook Inlet out of the Interior as early as 500 A.D., according to anthropologist William Workman as cited by Fall in his article "The Upper Inlet Tanaina" (1987). This arrival date is also supported by linguistic information, according to Kari. This timing would have put the Dena'ina in the upper inlet more than 1,000 years earlier than some other scholars have speculated. The upper inlet Dena'ina were a distinct group and arrived on Cook Inlet much earlier than the Dena'ina who later populated the Kenai Peninsula.

Archaeological artifacts found in the area indicate that the Alutiiq of Kodiak or Prince William Sound probably frequented the upper inlet as well, and perhaps were displaced by the Dena'ina. The Dena'ina apparently adapted tools for the marine environment, perhaps borrowing technology from the Alutiiq including the kayaklike baidarka. While the Kodiak Alutiiq would have come in by water, the Prince William Sound Alutiiq would have traversed Portage Glacier. Dena'ina lore includes a story about one of the last battles against the Alutiiq who came over the glacier and raided an upper inlet Dena'ina village, according to a story told by Shem Pete. The Alutiiq kidnapped a Dena'ina chief's daughter, and were on their way home when Dena'ina warriors caught them pulling their boats from the water at Campbell Point. The Dena'ina killed all but a couple of the Alutiiq men, who were sent back to report what had happened.

The Dena'ina were the only Alaskan Athabaskans to live along saltwater. They found the upper inlet rich in food. They hunted beluga whales and adapted freshwater river fishing methods to the inlet's extreme tides. The Knik Dena'ina hunted caribou in upper Ship Creek, and other wild game such as moose and beaver in the swampy muskeg and spruce forests of the Anchorage bowl, and sheep and goats on the mountainsides.

An important trading place for the upper inlet Dena'ina was at Point MacKenzie, across from Ship Creek. The Knik Dena'ina would take sheep and other food items in boats to Point MacKenzie to trade for hooligan and other items brought by the Susitna Dena'ina. The Ahtna people from the Copper River region on the eastern side of the Chugach Mountains would also come to Point MacKenzie to trade. The Ahtna and the Knik Dena'ina were closely associated and traded frequently with each other along a trail up the Matanuska River valley and through the mountains, a route later followed by the Glenn Highway.

According to Shem Pete, the distance between Point MacKenzie and Ship Creek used to be narrow, like a river. People on either side could share their ulus for cutting up fish, tossing them across the water to each other. "I heard that from those old people," Pete said.

The mouth of Ship Creek was an important summer fish camp for several Eklutna families. Called *Dgheyay Kaq'*, or Stickleback Mouth, it was a "good place to save ourselves from starvation," Shem Pete recalled. Needlefish, or stickleback, swam in with the spawning king salmon, some of the first fish to return in the spring. "No one went to bed at this season, they say," said Pete. "They may have been starving and may have barely survived (the winter). At that *Dgheyay Leht* (Ship Creek) we save ourselves nicely. That is the only place like this...."

A short distance north of Ship Creek, the Dena'ina erected a dipnet platform made of logs at a place called *Tak'at*.

Point Woronzof, or *Nuch'ishtunt*, meaning

"place protected by the wind," was another important summer fish camp, with smokehouses and a dipnet platform. It was used by Dena'ina from Knik, Susitna and the Matanuska area until the mid-'40s, according to Shem Pete. Families also spent summers at fish camp on the west shore of Fire Island, which Dena'ina lore says used to be a basket in the sky of frozen clouds until it was blown into the water and turned into Fire Island, or *Nutil'iy*, meaning "object that stands in the water."

Among the many other Dena'ina place names that Shem Pete related were *Chanshtnu*, meaning Grass Creek, a place where people used to fish for king salmon. Whites apparently pronounced it as Chester Creek, and the name stuck.

Although the Russians were the first known Europeans to have contact with any of Alaska's Natives as early as 1741, it was English sailor Capt. James Cook who first encountered the upper inlet Dena'ina when he sailed into "Cook's River" in 1778. He met two men in baidarkas, perhaps Alutiiq hunters, suggested Joan Townsend in 1965. The next day, Cook was visited by Natives in canoes with double-bladed paddles, like those used with baidarkas, signaling with a leather "frock" that they wanted to trade. In the days that followed, Cook encountered three more groups of Natives who he determined were Eskimos from Prince William Sound. Fall cites Frederica de Laguna in his suggestion that these people were more likely Dena'ina who lived nearby.

The Russians later pursued the fur trade into the inlet, although the Dena'ina resisted their control. Oral tradition includes stories about massacres of Russians at Tyonek. In 1843, a Russian detachment made a disappointing

reconnaissance of the Susitna River. The Dena'ina population had been severely reduced by smallpox in the late 1830s. Their population was estimated by the Russians in 1845 to be only 816, about half the number the Russians had counted a decade earlier.

United States purchase of Alaska brought traders to open stores at Tyonek about 1875 and to Knik in 1882. The Dena'ina trapped and traded furs with the store owners. By the early 1880s, cannery ships began sailing into the upper inlet to fish for salmon and trade with the Dena'ina for furs. Starting in the late 1880s, white prospectors were looking for gold up the Susitna and Matanuska rivers. Tyonek became a major supply point, and military expeditions began mapping the valleys. Dena'ina were hired as guides, packers and letter carries and some of them used their boats to carry mail between Knik and the gold rush settlements of Sunrise and Hope on Turnagain Arm.

In 1914, a survey team landed at Ship Creek to chart a route for the government's new railroad. Shem Pete, about 14, and his mother had been bear hunting in Talkeetna that spring. He killed 14 black bears and prepared their meat and fur to take to fish camp. They rowed their dory from the mouth of the Susitna River across the inlet toward Anchorage and saw tents on top of the hill. "Lots of tents," recalled Shem Pete. "And they burn and cut the trees. It's full of smoke, fire, nighttime. They like to work the nighttime. It's too hot day time, June month, so a lot of people working. And I work in the restaurant. For about two weeks. And they play cards. Lots of gambling in the tent.

"We go back to Susitna in the dory. We tell the story, 'We see lots of white people. There's smoke all over in Anchorage there now....'" ●

Anchorage began unofficially as a tent city on Ship Creek flats in 1915 when rumors that President Woodrow Wilson would select a western route for construction of a federal railroad from Seward to Alaska's Interior were confirmed. In July 1915, lots surveyed on a forested tableland shown here on the right comprised the official townsite. (Photo No. 74-27, Helen Van Campen Col., Archives, University of Alaska Fairbanks)

visiting the area in 1794, renamed "River Turnagain" Turnagain Arm. More than a half century later, the U.S. Coast & Geodetic Survey labeled the northern waterway Knik Arm, from a Native word meaning "fire," that was applied to Dena'ina (Tanaina) Indians living along the arm's north shore. The mountains skirting the eastern border of the lowland were known by another Native word, Chugach.

Today this lowland forms the heart of the Anchorage bowl, the base of which gently slopes from the mountains to the sea, broken only by ridges of glacial moraine and by a few streams that follow the channels of the glaciers. One of these streams is Ship Creek.

Few whites were living in this bowl when Anchorage was born, and those few settlers likely would have been spared the population deluge that was about to fall on them were it not for the Alaska Railroad. President Woodrow Wilson had authorized construction of a federal railroad in 1915 when government policy sought to open for development resources in the Matanuska Valley and in Alaska's Interior. Alaskans were concerned about the growing power of the Morgan-Guggenheim business empire that already owned the Copper River and Northwestern Railroad from Cordova to the rich copper lodes of the Wrangell Mountains and hoped to expand its control of Alaska's resources. Other, less well-financed companies had tried to build a railroad along the "western" route from tidewater at Seward on Resurrection Bay to Alaska's Interior, but it took authorization from the president and appropriations from Congress to get the job done.

The work of building the railroad fell to the newly created Alaska Engineering Commission (AEC), headed by railroad builder William C. Edes, chairman; geologist Thomas Riggs, who would later govern the Alaska Territory; and Lt. Frederick Mears. When an AEC surveying party arrived at Ship Creek in 1914, they found a handful of cabins spread out along the north side of the creek. The J.D. Whitneys, Keith McCullough, Jack and Nellie Brown, Jimmy and Nellie St. Clair, and Thomas Jeter were already living in the area.

Jimmy St. Clair was a prospector and freighter who married Nellie after meeting her in Seward. In 1911 the Whitneys moved to Ship Creek. Bud and Daisy Whitney had arrived in Alaska late the previous century and followed the mining camps. Bud, from Montana, continued prospecting and freighting after the couple built a cabin near the St. Clairs. The following year two forest rangers

A successful ice fishing outing on DeLong Lake can produce rainbow trout or landlocked salmon. (Danny Daniels)

assigned to Chugach National Forest settled along Ship Creek, Jack Brown and his wife, Nellie, and Keith McCullough. A Cordova schoolteacher named Florence later caught McCullough's eye and the couple were married. Mrs. McCullough became one of the first schoolteachers in the infant Anchorage. Thomas Jeter, a bachelor, had moved to Ship Creek in 1908. When he refused to sell his property to the AEC, the government took it by eminent domain. The only other buildings of record in the Ship Creek area were a log cabin designed as a saloon and roadhouse in 1906 by Hitchkock and Weiremen, and George Palmer's warehouse along the shore of Cook Inlet about three miles north of the mouth of the creek.

Edes, Riggs and Mears left Alaska the fall of 1914, ordering a small work force to stay behind to build a mess hall and hospital at Ship Creek. The trio was operating on optimism at this time, because President Wilson would not announce his choice of a railroad route until the following

Anchorage

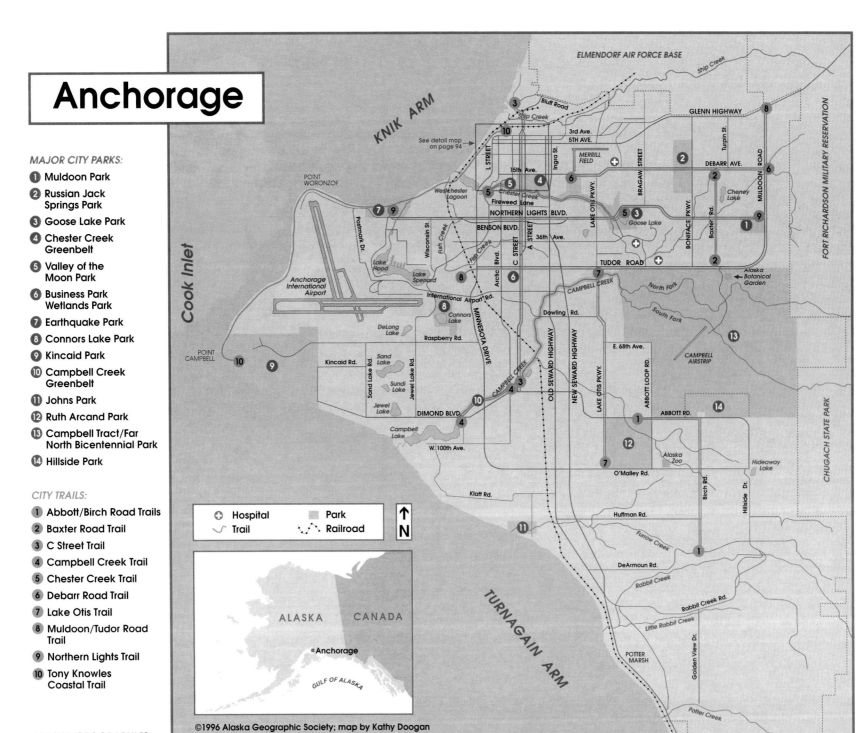

MAJOR CITY PARKS:

1. Muldoon Park
2. Russian Jack Springs Park
3. Goose Lake Park
4. Chester Creek Greenbelt
5. Valley of the Moon Park
6. Business Park Wetlands Park
7. Earthquake Park
8. Connors Lake Park
9. Kincaid Park
10. Campbell Creek Greenbelt
11. Johns Park
12. Ruth Arcand Park
13. Campbell Tract/Far North Bicentennial Park
14. Hillside Park

CITY TRAILS:

1. Abbott/Birch Road Trails
2. Baxter Road Trail
3. C Street Trail
4. Campbell Creek Trail
5. Chester Creek Trail
6. Debarr Road Trail
7. Lake Otis Trail
8. Muldoon/Tudor Road Trail
9. Northern Lights Trail
10. Tony Knowles Coastal Trail

Hospital   Park   Trail   Railroad

©1996 Alaska Geographic Society; map by Kathy Doogan

spring. But pioneers are nothing if not optimistic, and a tent camp accommodating several hundred had already sprouted beneath the bluff on the creek's north flank before the presidential selection was publicized. That bluff is now known as Government Hill, and it was on this north side that the AEC set up its headquarters. As an early writer, quoted in *Patterns of the Past* (1986), described the scene: "The paraphernalia of the woodsman and the hardy pioneer had to suffice, and a thousand tents, in the beginning, as white as Alaska's snows, made the town site resemble an army camp." According to the book's author, Michael Carberry, "By June, more than 2,000 souls packed the short-lived settlement."

Why did the AEC choose for their construction head-quarters a site with a practically non-existent harbor subject to siltation and widely fluctuating tides, and a creekside land base that consisted primarily of feet upon feet of mud? First, the site was one third of the way to Fairbanks, the northern terminus of the main line. Second, the plateaus on either side of Ship Creek allowed plenty of room for expansion of the camp and anticipated town. Third, and perhaps most important, Ship Creek lay on a straight line and an easy grade to the Matanuska coal fields, one of the rallying cries for constructing the railroad in the first place.

In time, the Ship Creek camp would become head-quarters for all operations of the railroad, but initially the project was divided into three regions, the southern in charge of Edes and centered at Seward, the middle under Mears headquartered at Ship Creek, and the northern under Riggs, at first operated from Fairbanks, and later Nenana. As construction progressed, the southern and middle segments were combined at Anchorage in 1917.

While the railroad pushed north and south from Anchorage, the tent camp mushroomed, and became a health hazard. Garbage was dispatched on the outgoing tide, and potable water cost 5 cents a bucket. But AEC commissioners feared sewage was leaking into the water supply. And the tent city was getting in the way of railroad operations.

The solution lay in platting a townsite, surveying and auctioning off lots and planning for the orderly growth of a new community on the tableland south of Ship Creek. Work crews cleared 240 acres, divided into 121 blocks that were partitioned into twelve 50-foot-by-140-foot lots. The lots were to be auctioned with a minimum bid of $25. Lots along the commercial heart of 4th Avenue required a higher minimum bid. Andrew Christensen, an employee of the General Land Office, supervised the auction. He also made a rousing sales pitch on behalf of the federal government, assuring potential buyers that the government had great plans to put money and energy into developing the

Heather Daniels hoes the soil in her family's garden. From the size of the vegetables behind her, the Daniels family appears to have a magic touch. Actually, potatoes, carrots, cabbage, cauliflower, broccoli, squash, onions and some other vegetables grow quite well in Anchorage gardens. (Danny Daniels)

ABOVE: *A temporary tent city sprung up along the banks of Ship Creek in summer 1990 when Anchorage celebrated its 75th anniversary. (Steve McCutcheon)*

RIGHT: *This statute of Capt. James Cook overlooks Ship Creek flats and Cook Inlet from Resolution Park at 3rd Avenue and L Street. (Harry M. Walker)*

territory. Christensen's enthusiasm spurred bidders. When the sale closed on July 18, 655 lots had earned a little less than $150,000 for government coffers. Reserves were set aside for a school, federal and city buildings, for parks and cemeteries. In addition, since prostitution was a fact of life, but not allowed, at least on paper, within the townsite, city planners tried to confine illicit activity to an area south of 6th Avenue.

The town's first newspaper, the *Cook Inlet Pioneer*, was established in June as the weekly *Knik News*. By September it was published daily, and later evolved into the *Anchorage Daily Times*. The *Pioneer* immediately pushed for a school because as it pointed out: "If we are to retain families — and they compose the backbone of any community — we must provide the children with adequate school facilities."

The residents had to settle the question of a name for the townsite and elect a school board. Both would be decided in an election held the following month.

Several names were proposed for the new city, some of which were already in use and some of which were championed by specific advocates: Ship Creek, Knik

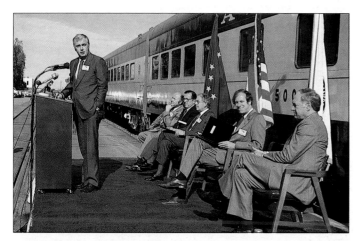

LEFT: *U.S. Sen. Frank Murkowski addresses a crowd at the official transfer of the Alaska Railroad from the federal government to the state in July 1984. The state bought the railroad for $22 million, signaling the end of federal ownership of the line that spurred the founding of Anchorage. With Sen. Murkowski on the platform are U.S. Sen. Ted Stevens (seated, second from left) and Alaska Gov. Bill Sheffield (next to Sen. Stevens). (Steve McCutcheon)*

BELOW: *In the 1990s, the Alaska Railroad built a new headquarters on Ship Creek flats, near where the railroad had its original district headquarters in 1915. (Steve McCutcheon)*

A winter sun shines through fog at the municipal boat dock near the outlet to Ship Creek. (Danny Daniels)

Anchorage, Ship Creek Landing, Matanuska, Alaska City, Winalaska, Gateway, Lane, Anchorage, Terminal, Homestead, Woodrow. The voters cast a majority for Alaska City, but they didn't reckon with the U.S. Post Office, which, shortly after President Wilson selected the route, designated the new camp Anchorage. The new post office opened in April 1915, with Roydon Chase as the first postmaster.

The same election gave Anchorage a school board, with Mrs. M.T. Normile as the first director, but the town as yet had no school. Anchorage was still managed by the AEC and residents would not receive patent to their land for five years. Thus, real estate could not be taxed and there was no money to build a school. Residents could petition for $1,000 school operating funds, but the AEC commissioners realized only they had enough money to actually build a school, which they did in 1915. Residents were handicapped by the inability to tax for almost another two years. On March 3, 1917, Congress passed a bill allowing territorial legislatures to establish schools and collect taxes for their support. The Pioneer School served until 1917 when Anchorage Public School was erected.

With the lots sold, the AEC ordered the Tent City dwellers to get off their creekside reserve and move to the new townsite. Businesses and residents moving from Tent City to the new townsite had to take C Street, the only road that ran from the plateau to the creek valley. Christensen Drive was later punched through on a curve because of the steepness of the bluff.

LEFT: *Frank M. Reed and Willard Nagley visit the modern-day tent city set up along Ship Creek to celebrate the town's anniversary. Frank came to Anchorage in 1916. His father was a miner who had been in Nome and decided to move his family to Anchorage. Frank's older brother was born in Nome; Frank was born in Seattle and came north when suitable housing was available in the new town. His dad continued to be involved in mining in the Cache Creek district north of Anchorage. Reed Sr. then moved to Anchorage, where he became active in city government. The family owned the Anchorage Hotel, and in the late 1920s, Reed Sr. established the city's first power plant at Eklutna. After college, Frank M. Reed was a banker in Anchorage for many years. Willard Nagley is from a pioneer mining family in the Talkeetna area. (Steve McCutcheon)*

BELOW: *Despite the "get-out-of-my-way" approach to driving displayed by some Anchorageites, many drivers show special courtesy to the wildlife that crosses their path. (Alaskana Photo-Art)*

Now that Anchorage had a townsite and the commissioners had cleared settlers from their lands, the AEC could focus on building and running a railroad. But they still had official charge of the town. So the AEC formed a Land and Industrial Department to supervise non-engineering and non-construction matters. J.A. Moore became the temporary townsite manager and J.G. Watts the townsite engineer.

The AEC continued providing essentials for the new town. The commission carried passengers on its construction trains for 6 cents a mile. By September, telephone and telegraph connected Anchorage and Seward; the connection with Fairbanks had to wait until 1920. In 1917, $1.00 could buy a caller three minutes long distance between Anchorage and Seward. Plans were laid to handle sanitation, fire control, a water system. The AEC built a hospital for its workers and the townsfolk. By 1916 the town had begun work on a power plant. Good thing, too, because Andrew Christensen estimated Anchorage's population in fall 1916 as 4,500.

By 1919, the AEC had completed work on a dock at Ship Creek. The dock spelled the end of the lightering services that had ferried passengers and cargo from ships anchored in the inlet to the landing. The townspeople hoped the dock would spur development of a full-scale port at Anchorage to encourage lower shipping prices, but when it was no longer needed for railroad construction, the AEC turned the dock over to local salmon canneries, thus excluding public use. The commission wanted to keep railroad revenues as high as possible by requiring the public to land their ocean cargo at Seward and ship it by rail the 114 miles to Anchorage. Cheaper transportation direct to a local dock would hinder their efforts.

Aspects of the seamier side of life kept pace with the growing population. Despite strictures handed out during the townsite auction that no property could be used for "illicit purposes," bootlegging, gambling and prostitution thrived. Pioneer Frank M. Reed, who came to Anchorage in 1916, recalled in 1995 that as a youngster he at one time had cornered the market on bottles needed by the bootleggers. His parents, Frank I. and Pauline H. Reed, owned the Anchorage Hotel, which his mother managed. Young Frank collected bottles that had been discarded by hotel guests, washed them and sold them to the bootleggers for 35 cents a dozen, washed. He was paid less for unwashed bottles. Frank would store his bottles in the hotel's furnace room, where they could be taken out the 3rd Avenue door. One time Frank became so busy with his chores at the hotel and with playing that he never quite had time to wash the

The start of Alaska's famed Iditarod Trail Sled Dog Race occurs the first weekend in March on 4th Avenue. The race resumes the following day at the Wasilla airport north of Anchorage, and runs for more than 1,000 miles to Nome, following a trail used in pioneer days by prospectors, miners and mushers. (Cary Anderson)

RIGHT: *The Anchorage Museum of History and Art, part of the Project 80s construction program paid for in large part by revenue generated from oil development, stands at the corner of 7th Avenue and A Street. In addition to exhibits from the museum's permanent history and art collections, the facility houses traveling exhibits and has a restaurant and gift shop. (Danny Daniels)*

LOWER RIGHT: *The Oscar Anderson house and children's play equipment attract visitors to Elderberry Park at the foot of 5th Avenue. A pioneer businessman, Anderson lived in this house, thought to be one of the first residences completed after the townsite auction. The house is open for tours at scheduled hours. (Danny Daniels)*

bottles. He kept stashing them in the furnace room and his collection grew. Finally taxi driver Chauncey Peterson hailed him, asking if he had any bottles. Chauncey offered 50 cents a dozen, unwashed. Young Frank made a deal with the driver, and helped load the taxi up to its windows four times as the bottles were ferried to a new site. The taxi could only be loaded to the level of the windows because bootlegging was illegal and Peterson didn't want officials to see his load. Frank learned an important lesson in the economics of supply and demand, one of many lessons that stood him in good stead when as an adult he became an Anchorage banker.

Legitimate commerce grew, and leisure activities also increased with the expanding population. Dashing Joe Spenard could be seen driving around town in his City Express Ford. Spenard operated a resort on Lake Spenard, and gave his name to the first suburb nourished by the growing city. The resort offered swimming in summer, skating in winter. Music and dancing in a lakeshore pavilion enlivened the evenings. Concrete sidewalks were poured for a few blocks along 4th Avenue, and one of the first admonitions of city fathers was that dog sleds and teams were to stay off the sidewalks.

Among the early cultural lights in Anchorage was photographer and artist Sydney Laurence. After a distinguished career in Europe, Laurence was attracted by the frontier atmosphere of Alaska and came to Anchorage in the teens after stays in Cordova and Valdez. He opened a photo studio in the Carrol Building on 4th Avenue in 1915. A year later he returned to painting, focusing on Mount McKinley, and moved into the Anchorage Hotel where he had his home and studio for many years. Laurence died in Anchorage in 1940, but his paintings have grown in reputation and cost and are now considered among the premier art to come out of Alaska.

The town continued to solidify its status on the frontier, but its population declined when World War I drew men and resources away from the railroad project. Estimates placed Anchorage's population near the end of 1917 at 3,928. By 1920 the figure had fallen to 1,856. But enough of the line was finished that the U.S. Post Office awarded its winter mail contract to the railroad rather than have the mail carried north from Valdez on the Richardson Highway.

By late 1920, Anchorage's position as a transportation center was enhanced even further. According to William H. Wilson in *Railroad in the Clouds* (1977), "On December 4 the railroad established through service over the 470 miles of main line, four days from Seward to Fairbanks with night layovers at Anchorage and Deadhorse (now Curry, mile 248.5) and McKinley Park (mile 348)."

This may not seem like much, but just three years earlier the trip from Seward to Anchorage or Seward to Fairbanks, demanded a marathon journey. Before the railroad, most travelers reached Anchorage by water, a journey of one day. Overland, a speedy trip took 35 hours, and most took much longer. Travel to Fairbanks could turn into a nightmare. In summer the itinerary called for waiting at Seward for a ship to Valdez, and continuing by car or wagon along the Richardson Highway to Fairbanks. During other seasons, travelers embarked at Seward for Cordova, rode the Copper River and Northwestern Railroad to Chitina, and continued by whatever means possible, wagon, car, sled or all three. Nenana, construction headquarters for the Fairbanks Division, lay another 60 miles down the Tanana River and could only be reached by boat or sled until 1919. The entire journey required at least five long days.

By the late teens, Anchorage had matured enough that the AEC thought it was about time for the townsfolk to manage their own affairs. ■

Bill and Lilian Stolt

By Charles P. Wohlforth

Editor's note: *Charles is a free-lance writer and a member of the Anchorage Municipal Assembly. He is a former reporter for the* Anchorage Daily News.

At 95, Bill Stolt is still quick with a story and a joke, so when Anchorage Mayor Rick Mystrom called to ask him to share the stage at his inauguration in 1994, Stolt told him the story about how when he was mayor, the salary was a dollar a year — and even that was never actually paid. Mystrom, who gets $107,000 a year, picked up on the joke by preparing a framed dollar to give to the former mayor as a surprise at the inauguration. Stolt, not to be outdone before an audience of more than 2,000 at the Alaska Center for the Performing Arts' Atwood Concert Hall, shot back to Mystrom, "Where's the interest?"

The interest after 50 years would be considerable, but still wouldn't come close to compensating Stolt for his contributions to the city during his time as a public servant. He created Municipal Light and Power, the city's electric utility, and upgraded its service just in time for the boom that hit Anchorage in World

Former Mayor Bill Stolt and his wife, Lilian, have been residents of Anchorage since the town was in its infancy. Bill was mayor in the early 1940s, when the town was experiencing the boom brought on by the defense buildup of World War II. (Courtesy of Bill and Lilian Stolt)

War II. Then he led the city through the worst of the war, sending his family south to avoid the danger of a Japanese invasion or shortages caused by severed supply lines.

In those days, the mayor's office was Stolts' electrical store on 4th Avenue and the mayor's secretary was his wife, Lilian, working in the front of the store. When territorial Gov. Ernest Gruening came in to see Mayor Stolt one day, Lilian says, "I didn't know he was the governor, so I said, 'Go look for him. He's in the back somewhere.'"

Stolt met frequently in those days with Gen. Simon Bolivar Buckner Jr., who was overseeing the transformation of the city into a military outpost. "Being mayor, they thought it would be a good idea if I set an example and sent the family out," he says.

In April 1942, Lilian gathered up their three children, then aged 2 to 11, and took them to Fairbanks to fly out. There was no commercial air service connecting Anchorage with Outside.

"You had to be fingerprinted each time you went in or out of the state, and all our mail was censored," Lilian recalls. "When I received his letters in St. Paul there were long parts blacked out." Anyone coming into town was searched for alcohol; the officials broke the bottles on the gangplank and poured the contents into Cook Inlet.

That December, when the military deemed Anchorage safe for women and children, the ship they came home in was escorted by a destroyer and a mine sweeper.

"We went into jewelry, gifts and souvenirs during the war years," Lilian says. "You couldn't get electrical supplies because they were all needed for the war effort."

In 1943, Bill Stolt stepped down as mayor, the biggest events of his life behind him, but he has remained active in Anchorage civic circles, among the friends he has known all his life here. As he lists off his past honors and titles, he finally gives up, saying, "I'm past-everything." He jokes, "I'll tell you, when your kids retire, that's when you know you're getting old."

Lilian is generally more serious.

"We've seen all this happen, since we've been here since we were young kids," she says. "Now it's a city of 250,000, and it was 2,500 when we came. So we're in the enviable position of seeing the entire history, and being able to tell about it — what we can remember."

Bill Stolt, third from left in front row, gathers with fellow workers in front of a rotary plow in 1928. With Stolt in the front row are, from left: Ben Fisher, Boiler Shop foreman; John Longacre, electrical engineer; Stolt, electrician; J.J. Iridale, chief clerk; Byron C. Elmes, traveling engineer; Ross Hale, master mechanic; Harry Dout, shop foreman; Ralph Nichols; Richard Lucason, general car foreman; and Jim Climie. Back row are: Walter F. Clarke, tinsmith; Fred Holdiman, machinist; W.H. (Bill) Cannon, boilermaker; Charles Sims, water service man; and Ralph Priddy. (Courtesy of Bill and Lilian Stolt)

They seem to be able to remember almost everything. Sitting in the living room of the house they built in 1953 on the shore of Bootlegger's Cove, where they maintain a large garden and work on various writing projects, the Stolts can look out their picture window and remember the city as it was before it was a city.

"There were Natives drying fish here in the summertime," Lilian says, gesturing out the window past the Tony Knowles Coastal Trail. "Right out here."

It was decades before Anchorage seemed a permanent city to many people, but the Stolts always believed in the town where they grew up. "When I was in city affairs, I predicted someday we'd have 10,000 people here," laughs Bill.

He was born in Boston in 1900, then carried as a young child back to Finland. Returning to the United States at age 10, Bill spoke no English, and his voice still carries a light Scandinavian accent. At age 13, his family moved to Juneau—Anchorage still hadn't been thought of yet— and four years later he arrived in Anchorage aboard a steamer.

"Anchorage was being built, and there was a lot of construction, so my stepfather wanted to move here," he says.

Bill was graduating in his high school class of two in 1920 when Lilian, then Lilian Rivers, arrived with her family, at age 13. Lilian's father, a railroad brakeman, had joined the new Alaska Railroad at a hiring office in Seattle. In such a small town, the two Finnish families knew each other, but Bill wasn't much interested in "just a high school girl" who wasn't allowed to date.

Both worked for the Alaska Railroad in the summer. Bill needed to earn the money to go to college. Lilian worked from age 16 in the paymaster's office, cutting checks for the men and keeping track of Bill's time card.

"A lot of us boys worked on the railroad in the summers," he says. "There was always work — in bridge gangs or construction."

He helped build bridges from Seward to Hurricane, and earned the nickname "little mule" for possessing physical strength out of proportion to his short stature.

Bill got his start in the repair career that would last him the rest of his life when the railroad bought a load of used typewriters and adding machines from Panama. He had learned to fix them at an office supply store. "I always had work, because I knew how to repair the typewriters," he says.

Lilian graduated from high school in 1924, in a class of three. She won a scholarship to Washington State University, which Bill was attending, but she planned to give it up and go to business college instead. He talked her out of it, and they graduated together in 1926.

Bill walked Lilian home from a dance at the Pioneer School House in 1923 or '24, but they didn't start dating until after they graduated from college. Bill, with a degree in electrical engineering, had job offers all over the territory. He took one with the railroad in Anchorage, while Lilian also returned to the railroad to work.

"We were having fun going fishing and dancing, so we didn't want to get married right away," she says.

Besides, the railroad had a policy of not employing married women. "When Lily got married, she would have been terminated," Bill says.

At the end of 1929 they married and moved to Seattle, where Bill worked for General Electric for two years. Then they returned to Alaska to work for a mining company in Willow for a year. Then, Bill says, "Lily and I decided, by God, let's try something on our own hook."

It was the worst of the Great

From 1915 through 1916, photographer and painter Sydney Laurence had his photo shop in the Carrol Building on 4th Avenue. In the 1930s, Bill and Lilian Stolt opened up their business next door to Laurence's former studio. (Courtesy of Bill and Lilian Stolt)

Lilian Stolt's father, Carl Rivers, bought this house at 618 8th Ave. in 1920 for $375. (Courtesy of Bill and Lilian Stolt)

Depression, but that didn't seem to matter. "We didn't know anything about it here," Bill says. In 1933, they opened the repair and electrical construction shop at 436 4th Ave., next door to Sydney Laurence's former photo shop.

Not long after, the painter needed lighting at his Anchorage Hotel shop.

"He had paintings, but he didn't have any money," Bill says. "He asked me — he needed work done — and he said he'd give me some paintings if I'd do it for him. And I said, 'I better help this boy, but I can hardly afford to do it myself.' He was a nice old guy, a sort of English gentleman."

They still have the paintings.

The family business slowly grew during the '30s, as the family, living in the upstairs apartment, grew. The Stolts added one employee at a time, always avoiding too much debt. "When we'd make a dollar we'd buy something, and when we'd make another dollar we'd buy something else," Bill says.

"We liked to be able to pay for something when we bought it," Lilian says.

It was that same practical outlook that got Bill Stolt into politics in 1938.

"People would come to me and say, 'Bill, I'd buy a waffle iron, but I can't get juice.' And I said, 'Why can't the city give them juice? They live this side of the cemetery.'"

The city electrician told him the town council had turned down any expansion.

"So I said, 'I'll run for council.' And when I

got elected, I told the city electrician — put in an order of poles and wires." The council went along with the plan to extend power all the way south to 9th Avenue.

"And then the war came, and we had a big boom, and it was a good thing we'd done it, because we'd be sitting in the dark," he says.

Bill's next project was to buy the electric generating utility from its owner, Frank I. Reed, whose son, Frank M. Reed, still lives a few blocks from the Stolts. But he ran into opposition from the coal company and other factions.

"I ran for mayor. I said, 'I'll put my head in as mayor and see if I can get it through.' There was no campaigning. I put my name in and forgot about it. That was it."

Lilian adds, "They just called and said, 'You're elected mayor.'"

After he was elected in 1941, Stolt got a bond issue on the ballot, it passed, and the utility now known as Municipal Light and Power came into the city's hands. Stolt says it makes sense for the utilities to belong to the city, because residents can benefit both from the service they provide and by putting profits

back into the city treasury. Former Mayor Tom Fink tried in 1993 to sell ML&P, and Stolt says, "That really griped me. I went to all that trouble to buy it and then he wants to sell it."

The years leading up to World War II had been quiet in Anchorage. In 1939, the population was still less than 5,000. Ten years later, it would be more than 30,000, as servicemen who came to defend Alaska came back to stay after the war was over.

The Stolts' family expansion finally forced them to move out of the apartment in the store. Bill has another story to go with the event.

"We had three children, and we couldn't fit in that little apartment," he says, so he bought a house at 211 E. 5th Ave. "I bought it from a guy who said, 'I started building this myself, but Anchorage isn't going to amount to anything. They're going to build a naval base out at Sitka, so I'm going to go down there and build a house.' Two weeks later, they unloaded the bulldozers down at the Whitney Dock to build the air base here."

After a lifetime here, the Stolts' feel their optimism about Anchorage has been vindicated. They're happy with the way the city turned out.

Lilian still meets with the "Mothers' Club" she joined in 1932, although the members are mostly great grandmothers now.

"I haven't got anybody — all the old guys are gone," says Bill.

But he still has friends among the younger generation, like George Sullivan, who was mayor from 1967 to 1982. "He's still a skookum guy," Sullivan says. "A great sense of humor. Every time he's called upon to say a few words, he's got a good story to tell." ●

Anchorage's Adolescence

After five years of federal oversight, residents of Anchorage had gotten used to having the government provide them with many services. But the AEC commissioners were more interested in running a railroad than a town. They pressured residents to set up their own government, which the townsfolk did, reluctantly, in late 1920. On November 23, Anchorage was incorporated. Lawyer Leopold David, who had already been in Alaska for more than 10 years and had been serving as U.S. Commissioner, was elected president of the city council and the first mayor. Among issues facing the first city government were better street lighting, the financing of a fire department and acquiring a fire truck. The city had taxing power and assessed levies on real and personal property, required a license for peddlers and passed an ordinance to control dogs and stray cattle.

Prostitution again became an issue, when a "prominent" but unnamed citizen appeared before the council proclaiming that the immoral status of the neighborhood between 6th and 9th avenues was corrupting neighborhood children. Illegal activities occupied much of the council's time, a situation made all the more imperative when chief of police, John J. Sturgis, was murdered before the council was yet three months old.

In some respects, issues occupying the council in the century's third decade still entangle the municipal assembly in the century's last decade. In early 1921 a curfew was adopted for children under 16. Citizens were reminded that they had to keep their sidewalks and alleyways clear, and

ordinances were approved regulating liquor and open gambling in pool halls and cigar stores. Fast driving also proved a vexing problem. According to city records, the chief of police was instructed to arrest "each and every driver of automobiles who exceeded the speed limit of eight miles per hour."

No doubt the most momentous departure from Anchorage's routine in the early 1920s was the visit of President Warren G. Harding, who had come north in 1923 to drive the golden spike at Nenana, commemorating completion of the railroad. Connecting Seward to Fairbanks by rail also meant a chance to add tourism to Anchorage's economic pie. Circle routes through Anchorage and on to Fairbanks and back down the Richardson Highway to Valdez, or by riverboat from Fairbanks down the Tanana River and up the Yukon to Whitehorse, then to tidewater at Skagway by way of the White Pass & Yukon rail line provided tourists with a glimpse of a good cross section of Alaska. Anchorage hotels, restaurants, transfer services and theaters looked to this traffic as a source of revenue.

Anchorage's leisure palate was well-fed also. Community theater and music, movies, parades, card-playing and sports helped pass the time. Ice skating, hockey, skiing and dog mushing took on a more formal routine with organization of a winter sports festival in the 1930s. Baseball, tennis and golfing on a nine-hole course augmented the hiking and swimming of summer. Fraternal and social organizations had taken hold early on. The Elks, Moose, Anchorage Women's Club and numerous others planned a full range of activities. The Masons built a lodge where the F.W. Woolworth store now stands in downtown Anchorage.

Anchorage missed out on the good times that spread throughout the Lower 48 in the 1920s. This occurred partly because the prosperity was fueled by commerce and manufacturing, slices of the economic pie not yet viable in Anchorage's small market, where citizens provided most of their own needs and population was declining. At the beginning of the decade, the town's population had shrunk to 1,856, mostly the result of downsizing on the railroad. At the time, Alaskans' only realistic trade commodities were salmon and gold, with furs and other fish products accounting for a much smaller trade.

Commercial salmon canning operations began at Anchorage in the 1920s. For the next several decades, at least eight companies operated canneries or fish processing plants at the port, although most were short-lived.

Completion of the railroad enhanced Anchorage's position as a supply and shipment center for miners. The town became the center for transshipment of gold from Iditarod and Willow mining areas. The Bank of Alaska displayed gold exhibits totaling thousands of dollars, and dog teams came through town hauling hundreds of thousands of dollars worth of gold bullion.

LEFT: *A containership is docked at the port of Anchorage, nestled at the base of Government Hill. In 1995, the port handled 1.5 million tons of general cargo and 10 million barrels of bulk petroleum. (Scott Darsney)*

BELOW: *Mail carrier Primula Babcock delivers to homes in west Anchorage. (Danny Daniels)*

Mining had been active in the Willow Creek district in the Talkeetna Mountains since just after the turn of the century, but operating in the rugged mountains was expensive because of shipping costs. Kathryn Cohen writes in *Independence Mine and the Willow Creek Mining District* (1982): "Freight costs in 1913 between Seattle and Ship Creek [Anchorage] ranged from $15 to $26 per ton. Passengers paid $55 for a one-way ticket. Transport by launch from Ship Creek to Knik cost passengers an additional $2, and freight rates averaged 30 to 40 percent of the charge from Seattle to Ship Creek. With a miner's wage averaging $3.50 a day, a one-way ticket from Seattle to Knik, accompanied by one ton of freight at $77, cost roughly a full month's wages." After the rail line was laid to Wasilla, mining supplies and equipment could be shipped to Seward or Anchorage and brought north on the train.

Mining offered settlers a chance to earn wages when times were lean, and families of miners lived in Wasilla or Anchorage and spent their incomes locally.

Mining also boosted a developing air industry in Anchorage. Flying people and equipment to the mines was even more efficient than taking the train. Wesley Earl Dunkle, superintendent of Willow Creek's Lucky Shot mine, bankrolled Seattle pilots Stephen Mills and Jack Waterworth, who moved to Anchorage and set up a flying school in the 1930s. In return, Dunkle received flying lessons and winter transportation to his mine.

Perhaps the greatest legacy of the 1920s and 1930s was the development of commercial air travel. Planes seemed the proper solution to traversing Alaska's vast distances and rugged terrain. Among the first commercial outfits was Anchorage Air Transports Inc. whose plane Anchorage No. 1 operated from an area south of town that had been cleared in 1923, first as a firebreak and later as a runway. The clearing, between 9th and 10th avenues, was the southern boundary of town. Noel Wien, one of four brothers who pioneered aviation in Alaska, had a J-One shipped by rail from Seward to Anchorage in June 1924. Wien and his mechanic W.B. Yunker put the plane together, which Wien flew the day after Independence Day to Fairbanks, following the rail line. This was the first flight from Anchorage to Fairbanks.

Russel Merrill was one of the first pilots for Anchorage Air Transports. An ex-Navy flyer, he came to Alaska in 1925. Two years later, he had teamed with G.E. "Ed" Young and Lyle Stanford to hire on as the first pilots for the fledgling airline. He was lost on a flight delivering

ABOVE: *The Stellers jay has expanded its range from the southeast into the Anchorage bowl in the last couple of decades. The species, which usually appears as a dark-gray-headed bird with a blue back, displays an iridescent blue body and blue-tipped crest when seen in good light. This species is the first recorded for Alaska and is named for George Steller, naturalist with Vitus Bering on his 1741 expedition usually credited with discovering Alaska. (Tim van Nest)*

ABOVE RIGHT: *The Musk Ox Producers' Co-op operates a shop on 6th Avenue where they market qiviut items made by village Natives. Qiviut is the soft underhair of the musk ox. The Co-op buys qiviut from the Musk Ox Farm in Palmer, and obtains other qiviut from the research station at the University of Alaska Fairbanks and from village women whom it hires to gather the qiviut from wild musk ox. The Co-op arranges to have the qiviut spun into yarn, then distributes it to village women who knit articles of clothing using traditional Native patterns. (Harry M. Walker)*

equipment to miners across Cook Inlet in 1929; the following year the Anchorage Women's Club suggested that the new airfield being laid out east of downtown be named in Merrill's honor.

About 1932 Star Air Service started in Anchorage when the two Seattle pilots Dunkle had lured north opened a flight school and airline. In 1934 it merged with McGee Airways — whose founder, Linious McGee, had a good head for business and frequently managed the company — to become Star Airlines, which later joined with several other airlines to become Alaska Star Airlines, shortening their name in 1944 to Alaska Airlines. Art Woodley got his start about the same time. Woodley Airways would grow into one of the largest in Alaska and eventually become part of Western Airlines. The late 1920s and 1930s was the era of the bush pilot, when Alaskans really looked to the airplane to solve transportation problems and government regulations had not yet caught up with the seat-of-the-pants but usually successful flying of the intrepid pilots and their mechanics.

"There is no question," wrote Archie Satterfield in *The Alaska Airlines Story* (1981), "that both Linious McGee and Star Air Service were major contributors in making Anchorage the major city in Alaska and in helping it overtake Fairbanks in the competition for business, government contracts and international attention. For several decades, Fairbanks had been the dominant city in the Interior due to the riverboat traffic and the railhead. The first airplanes operated out of Fairbanks, and the first airmail contract was granted to a Fairbanks-based pilot....

"But McGee and Star began making an impact on Alaskans' shopping habits. Their pilots became shoppers for families and roadhouse operators.... They brought safety pins, sewing machines, phonographs, diapers, window curtains, bandages, and everything else Anchorage residents were accustomed to buying downtown. They delivered merchandise ordered from Sears Roebuck catalogs that was shipped COD to Anchorage. The pilots or airlines paid the COD charges, then collected on delivery themselves....

"Robert B. Atwood, publisher of the *Anchorage Daily Times* who arrived in Alaska in 1935, was dependent on the bush pilots for his news from the Interior. He ran a regular 'airport,' or comings-and-goings column based almost entirely on reports from the pilots....

"Before long, airline employees were spending too much time shopping for the people in the Interior, so Star hired Lorene Harrison to go up and down Fourth Avenue every day filling the orders."

One of McGee's pet peeves was flying a plane that was not fully loaded. If there was no orthodox cargo to be flown,

McGee's pilots would find whatever commodity might be available and peddle it along the way. Pilot Johnny Moore once took this bartering skill to a new high when he traded a planeload of fresh celery for fox skins.

By 1930, Anchorage's population had increased to 2,736. Just as the town had not fully participated in the boom of the 1920s, it also did not sink as far as the rest of the country during the Depression of the 1930s. Compared to city dwellers Outside, Alaskans could and did produce most daily essentials, and the railroad continued to support the

Even though Anchorage has many hotels, rooms can be fully booked during the summer tourist season. Fortunately, bed and breakfasts have sprung up throughout the city, such as this one, The Lilac House, to accommodate the increased visitor traffic. (Danny Daniels)

bulk of the economy. Fishing and mining employed fewer workers, although President Franklin Roosevelt's pegging of the price of gold at $35 an ounce did bring stability and some renewed vigor to the gold mining industry by mid-decade.

Alaska participated to a limited extent in the public works programs initiated by the Roosevelt administration. But one federal program became a hallmark of the 1930s in the Anchorage area. In 1935 a contingent of agricultural colonists, mostly from the Midwest, arrived in Anchorage. The government provided the newcomers land and money to develop agriculture in the Matanuska Valley. As with most schemes, dreams and reality clashed. Many colonists turned about immediately or after some months, preferring

the known of their previous homelands to the uncertainty that faced them in the mountain-rimmed valley 30 miles from Anchorage. But some families stuck it out and prospered, especially when they switched from growing crops to raising dairy cows. They were joined by others. Eventually the colony had a firm clasp on its future, and the settlers added their wealth to a growing Anchorage economy.

By the end of the decade, Anchorage's outlook, if not booming, at least appeared promising. The railroad under the tutelage of Col. Otto Ohlson had operated in the black for some years. Speculation circulated that the government would be spending more money in the area building military installations. The town's railroad and air transportation systems were on a sound footing. Optimism was just beyond the threshold, and the Japanese were preparing for war. ∎

LEFT: *The tranquil campus of Alaska Pacific University, with its Waldron Carillon Belltower shown here, tops a knoll in eastcentral Anchorage, just east of the University of Alaska Anchorage campus. Built in 1972, the tower was funded by Arthur F. Waldron in honor of his wife, Edith. Waldron was a major supporter and early pioneer who, as chairman of the Committee of 100, traveled throughout the country in the 1950s raising funds to start the college. Founded as a Methodist school and formerly named Alaska Methodist University, Alaska Pacific University is a private, liberal arts institution supported partially by the United Methodist Church and other denominations. (Alissa Crandall)*

FACING PAGE: *Hot summer days draw swimmers to Goose Lake near East High School. The lake also has a nesting pair of Pacific loons, and is the best place in town for people to see this species. In fact, Anchorage is the largest city in North America with nesting loons. (Danny Daniels)*

In 1992 the Anchorage Daily News, *owned by the California-based McClatchy chain, emerged victorious in its long war with the* Anchorage Times. *In 1995 the* Daily News *proudly displayed a banner in celebration of 49 years of publishing in the 49th state. (Alaskana Photo-Art)*

world enable this shop to outfit women of this area as smartly as if they shopped on New York's Fifth Avenue."

Many of the city's dances and social events took place at the Elks Lodge. Cultural activities included concerts by the 50-piece symphony orchestra, the 100-voice community chorus and live theatrical productions. Youngsters could be tutored in the arts at Gertrude Mulcahy's charm school, or at several dance schools. Numerous chapters of national civic and fraternal organizations started, supplementing those already in existence.

The mid-1940s also found Anchorage with an active "Post-War Planning Committee" undertaking city improvements desperately needed by the growing town. One of the biggest needs was more dependable electrical power; outages occurred almost daily. In 1946, a salvaged oil tanker with a 5,400-kilowatt steam generator was dry-docked on the mud flats to supplement power from a diesel generator and a small hydroelectric plant at Eklutna.

Always fond of slogans — past ones included "Outlet on the Inlet" and "Seattle of Cook Inlet" — Anchorage now billed itself as "Air Crossroads of the World." The importance of aviation to Alaska had been reinforced by the war, and now Anchorage was poised to became a major civilian air hub. Seven commercial air carriers operated from Merrill Field, and in summer Lake Spenard buzzed with floatplanes. An estimated 60 percent of all civilian airplanes through Anchorage in summer were floatplanes. For four of the years from 1945 to 1950, Merrill Field outranked San Francisco and Los Angeles in civilian air traffic. For good reason, Anchorage was said to be "the most air-minded city in the world."

Anchorage's leaders saw the economic potential of air

ABOVE: *On weekends and long summer evenings, Anchorage residents head southeast along Turnagain Arm. If the winds are up, one of the main attractions of the drive is watching the wind surfers skimming the waters of Turnagain Arm near Beluga Point. (Alaskana Photo-Art)*

ABOVE RIGHT: *Canary vine and lithrum decorate the corner of this home on the Hillside. (Jill Shepherd)*

travel overseas, because of the city's location on the North Pacific rim, and began to promote the idea of international passenger flights to Asia. The Civil Aeronautics Board, which had its Alaska headquarters in Anchorage, decided to make Anchorage the hub for new international routes. Direct flights were established by Northwest Orient Airlines between Anchorage and Seattle, Anchorage and Minneapolis and from Anchorage to the Orient. In spring 1949, construction started on a new international airport.

In comparison, few improvements graced overland travel in and out of Anchorage. The Alaska Railroad went south to Seward and north to Fairbanks, a two-day trip with an overnight at the Curry Hotel or McKinley Park. Completed in the early 1940s, the only road out of town was the Glenn Highway, a two-lane gravel road to Palmer and on through the mountains to the Richardson Highway, and finally the military's Alaska Highway at Tok. The highways weren't always passable in winter, but at least Anchorage could say that it was connected by road to the contiguous states. Despite the fact that roads were few, cars were not. Between 1947 and 1951, the number of licensed automobiles in Anchorage jumped 280 percent, to more than 16,000, more than half the total number of cars in the territory, according to a book about Anchorage published in 1953 by the Alaska Development Board. The actual number of cars in the Anchorage area was closer to 25,000, counting those of the military and nonresidents.

In 1946, as Atwood was building a new home for his *Anchorage Daily Times* on 4th Avenue, Anchorage got a second newspaper. Norman Brown, a former *Times* reporter, started the *Anchorage News* as a community weekly. Within the year, he stepped up publication and made it into the evening *Anchorage Daily News*. The *News* would grow into an award-winning, hard-hitting morning paper, winning two Pulitzers for public service, and the two papers would eventually face off for survival in one of the nation's

hottest and last newspaper wars of the century. But during this period, the *News* posed little threat to the better-established *Times*.

The *Times* was an unflinching advocate for development of Anchorage, the railbelt and Alaska in general, reflecting the philosophy of its publisher and the business community. Its editorial campaigns figured into almost every major development, such as the establishment of the military installation at Anchorage and the relocation of federal offices to town. By the mid-1940s, more than a dozen federal agencies were headquartered in Anchorage and the town had become the defacto government capital for the territory. The Federal Bureau of Investigation moved its offices to Anchorage from Juneau, and the District Court relocated from Valdez. Government provided a large percentage of jobs.

Meantime, Atwood, Gov. Gruening and Bob Bartlett, the territorial delegate in Congress, decided the time had arrived to pursue statehood. The federal government owned 98 percent of the territory and was becoming increasingly meddlesome in the daily lives of Alaskans. And there was the continuing matter of the power held by

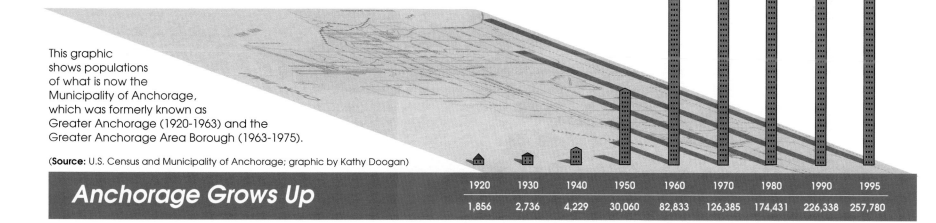

This graphic shows populations of what is now the Municipality of Anchorage, which was formerly known as Greater Anchorage (1920-1963) and the Greater Anchorage Area Borough (1963-1975).

(**Source:** U.S. Census and Municipality of Anchorage; graphic by Kathy Doogan)

Anchorage Grows Up

1920	1930	1940	1950	1960	1970	1980	1990	1995
1,856	2,736	4,229	30,060	82,833	126,385	174,431	226,338	257,780

Outside interests. In 1945, Congress acquiesced to Seattle salmon canners and refused to let the territory take control of its fisheries; the territory wanted to outlaw cannery fish traps, which were devastating the runs. So in 1946, Atwood and his friends formed the Alaska Statehood Association in Anchorage. Chapters formed in 10 communities, and the association published and distributed position papers promoting statehood before a territorial vote on the issue. Anchorage favored statehood, two to one, according to Evangeline Atwood in *Anchorage, Star of the North* (1982). Several prominent Anchorage leaders were appointed in 1949 to the Alaska Statehood Committee, formed by the legislature to promote statehood. Opponents to the move included the salmon canners, but also Alaska sourdoughs who feared higher taxes and those who thought the statehood boosters merely wanted to create their own self-serving aristocracy.

As the decade closed, Anchorage was still growing. But by 1948, government expenditures, largely due to the military slowdown, were the lowest since the war. Before the town could feel any effects, though, news arrived that the military would be doubling its forces in Alaska. Deteriorating relations with Russia put the territory on the front lines of the emerging Cold War, and Anchorage would be the headquarters. ■

ABOVE LEFT: *Anchorage firefighters stage a demonstration for area children. Busy fire and police departments tend to the needs of a growing city. (Alissa Crandall)*

LEFT: *Tlingit Esther Shea of Ketchikan demonstrates the making of a button blanket at an exhibit by Native artisans at the Anchorage Museum of History and Art. (Harry M. Walker)*

FACING PAGE: *The multiuse trail along the Chester Creek greenbelt crosses Northern Lights Boulevard near East High School. (Cary Anderson)*

Fur Rondy, A Winter Tradition

By L.J. Campbell

Every February, good-time sounds echo through Anchorage. Fireworks crackle against the night sky. Sled dogs yip-yip-yap, lunging to sprint on snowpacked trails. Fiddles spill reels and waltzes across a crowded dance floor. Hammers ping against chisels as artists carve 8-foot-tall snow blocks into figures. Ferris wheel and roller coaster churn frosty air with squealing, shrieking passengers. And amid piles of fur pelts an auctioneer chants "*going, going, gone.*"

These sounds are part of Anchorage Fur Rendezvous, the state's largest cold weather celebration. From its modest start some 60 years ago, Fur Rendezvous has grown into one of the nation's top 10 winter festivals with a budget of more than $1 million and estimated attendance of 300,000 people. Nearly 100 different events, activities, races and contests, many of them free, make up the festival schedule.

Throughout town for 10 days and nights in early February, in almost every place where

No festival is complete without fireworks. (Harry M. Walker)

crowds can gather, fun happens. Fur Rondy, as it's popularly known, packs a lineup designed to appeal to people of all ages and interests. In the most generic sense, Fur Rondy is like any other big city festival. It has a parade, a carnival, fireworks, a beauty pageant, lots of exhibits, arts and crafts shows, concerts, dances, sports tournaments and contests galore. But Fur Rondy comes with a twist, by virtue of

Anchorage's place in the North. Softball players play in snowshoes, grand prix cars race on icy streets, games include the Eskimo blanket toss, and children bundle warmly in gloves, hats and coats to brave freezing carnival rides. Sled dog races anchor the festival, and sled dog rides put visitors in the musher's sled. Fur Rondy's fireworks draw thousands of spectators who enjoy the show from inside warm, parked cars; Rondy's fireworks are the best of the year, since Anchorage's summer skies are hardly dark at all for July 4th displays.

But what has traditionally set Fur Rondy apart from other winter festivals is its fur auction. The festival's name comes from a trapping tradition, the rendezvous of fur trappers to trade and sell their winter harvests. Practiced for more than a century at French Canadian outposts, the fur rendezvous was a fixture among trappers of the American Rocky Mountains in the 1820s. Anchorage, built as a railroad town in 1915, arrived late to the fur trade, but as the town grew into a regional center, fur buying became part of the mix.

One of the first fur buyers in town was Isaac Koslosky, who ran a clothing store on 4th Avenue. He bought some furs outright and accepted others to settle grubstake debts from men who prospected in summer and trapped in winter. Most of the furs from Alaska ended up at auctions in Seattle and Canada, the big fur exchanges where manufacturers shopped for pelts. Some trappers sent their pelts directly to auction by mail, carried out by dog sled, riverboat and steamship. Other trappers dealt instead with local fur buyers, middlemen known in the trade as fur collectors. By the late 1920s, Anchorage was an important fur collection point for buyers who traveled by airplane to villages and trap lines and brought back bundles of pelts to put on the train to Seward for shipment to the Seattle Fur Exchange.

Finally in 1938, Anchorage got its own fur auction. It was held during the Anchorage Winter Sports Festival, which was thereafter

known as Anchorage Fur Rendezvous. Vernon Johnson, a retired butcher who is considered the "father of Fur Rondy," recalls the festival's origins, which had more to do with hockey than trapping.

It used to be in the 1930s that Fairbanks held a winter carnival, a popular affair each March that drew people by train from Anchorage. In 1935, a group of men from the Anchorage Amateur Athletic Association decided to form a team to play in the carnival's hockey tournament. The 4As, as they called the

association, promoted baseball in summer, so hockey was a new challenge. "A lot of the guys had never played hockey before. They could hardly skate," remembers Johnson, now 86, who was president of the association at the time. For that first tournament game, the newly formed Anchorage team rigged up uniforms consisting of sweatshirts and basketball trunks and long wool socks pulled up over *Saturday Evening Post*s, which they rolled up and taped to their legs as shin guards.

They were surely a motley-looking crew as

A flooded baseball diamond at the old Mulcahy Park became a public ice skating rink each winter. In this mid-1930s photo, Vernon Johnson, credited with founding Fur Rondy, kneels at extreme right. The other team members are: from left, front row, Buddy Minano, Woody Hile, Frank Brandt and Leonard Cappstick; back row, Percy Pugh, Stanley McCutcheon, Floyd Truesdell, J. Vic Brown Jr., Mott Leek, Mr. Wagner and Grover Fireoved. (Courtesy of Steve McCutcheon)

they piled out of the train onto the Chena River ice, where a cleared oval lined with foot-high boards served as the rink. "We spent most of

LEFT: *This "udderly" fantastic team enjoys the costume competition at the Miners and Trappers Ball. (Harry M. Walker)*

BELOW LEFT: *This grumpy-looking fellow took first place in the woodcarving competition. (Harry M. Walker)*

BELOW: *Wonder how the Big Leaguers would do during the snowshoe softball competition? (Harry M. Walker)*

the time chasing pucks over the boards in the snow," Johnson recalls. Between games, they'd head to a nearby brewery on the river to drink beers and warm their toes. They played heartily but were no match for the Canadians from Whitehorse, who dominated the tournament.

The train ride back to Anchorage took 18 long hours behind a rotary snow plow. But the excitement of the game and glow of camaraderie held forth and as the train chugged through Broad Pass, the hockey players decided that Anchorage needed its own winter festival. They determined then to organize something for the following February, to break up the dull, dreary month.

Plans for the first Anchorage Sports Festival

got underway that fall. The 4As erected some sideboards around a low spot at Mulcahy Park, then at the corner of 6th and C streets, and flooded it for a hockey rink. A couple of fellows manned the rink, to keep the ice smooth and collect a small fee from public users to pay for maintenance. The gym at the town's only elementary-high school, between 5th and 6th avenues where the Alaska Center for the Performing Arts stands today, was readied for a basketball tournament. A ski jump went up on the hill overlooking Chester Creek, and some trails were groomed for cross-country ski racers. Bleachers were put up around the hockey rink. Everything was in place when out-of-town competitors and spectators started arriving, most of them booked into homes for the week of competitions. Three dollars bought a season's pass to all the events. It was quite a success, Johnson says.

With the first festival behind them, organizers started looking toward the next. Fire chief Tom Bevers, who had been reading about fur rendezvous tradition, suggested adding a fur auction to the festival as a way to get more people to come into town. That year with the addition of the fur auction, the festival name was changed to Fur Rendezvous and was turned over to the Chamber of Commerce to run. Fur Rondy buttons became the season's token pass; today buttons are still Rondy currency and the old buttons are valued collector pieces.

The fur auction soon became the festival's centerpiece. The auction would last for several days with the furs displayed around downtown for interested buyers to inspect, recalls photographer Steve McCutcheon who moved to Anchorage as a child with his parents in 1915. Another observer remembers how the smell of

ABOVE: *Stony competes in the middle-weight class of the World Championship Dog Weight Pull. (Harry M. Walker)*

RIGHT: *Teamwork carries this ski-jorer along during the Rondy competition. (Alaskana Photo-Art)*

furs permeated hotel lobbies downtown, as trappers piled their pelts on the floors.

The auction further reinforced Anchorage's role in the Alaska fur trade, bringing fur clothing manufacturers to town. One of these was David Green, a furrier who had shops in Ketchikan, Sitka, Juneau and Fairbanks.

LEFT: *The premier event at Fur Rondy is the World Championship Sled Dog Race. Here Canadian musher Terry Streeper starts down 4th Avenue in one of three heats to decide the winner. (Harry M. Walker)*

ABOVE: *Speed skaters compete at Mulcahy Park. (Harry M. Walker)*

Through the 1930s, he had visited Anchorage as a traveling collector, buying furs on plane trips into the Bush. Fine lynx and red fox pelts came out of the Copper Valley region while the western Alaska wetlands were known for their beaver and muskrats, wolverine and wild mink. Valued pelts from the Kenai Peninsula included a wild mink with unusually fine, silky fur. In the 1950s, Green closed his other stores and opened his Anchorage business on 4th Avenue, where his sons, master furriers Perry and Jerry, continue the family business, participating in Fur Rondy by sponsoring a fur fashion show and fur bikini contest.

For years, the actual fur auction was conducted by Hess Brothers Auctioneers. Andy Hess had taken over running the fur auction in 1961, when the event became too much for downtown fur dealers to continue. The auction was held then on 4th Avenue, outside what is now the log cabin visitors center. The next year, the auction moved to a location on 3rd Avenue near the carnival, its site for most years since except for a few times when it was held indoors at the Sullivan Arena. James took charge of the auction when his dad died.

Conducting the fur auction was a major undertaking. The Hesses advertised months in advance for consignments, built stands to display the furs for auction, and handled hundreds of raw pelts that arrived by mail or were delivered in person to the Hess auction barn on Muldoon Road. (In recent years, the state Dept. of Fish and Game has supplied the bulk of the furs, which are illegally harvested pelts confiscated by law enforcement officials.) Then on the day of the auction, the pelts had to be trucked to the site and set up for sale. The sale itself lasted most of a day, after which the books had to be settled and the consignors paid.

Both Andy and James loved the fur auction, said James' wife, Bernardine. They enjoyed seeing the variety of people who attended, she said, and they'd arrive early and linger to visit long after the last pelt was sold. The bear pelts always elicited the most, and biggest, stories, she said, "especially if the person who shot it was there. Or there'd be a fellow who knew a friend who shot it or was mauled by it. Always the bear stories...."

James Hess died in September 1994, and in 1995 Fur Rondy was without a fur auction for the first time. The Hess family decided to pass on responsibility for future auctions and in 1996, a company called Sourdough Productions was in charge.

Fur Rondy also has become known for its world championship sled dog races. Like the fur auction, sled dog racing was added to attract yet another group of people to Anchorage. In the early years of Fur Rondy dog races, most of the competitors came from Alaska's Native villages. But today, mushers come from urban Alaska, Canada and the Lower 48 to compete. The Fur Rondy world championship sled dog races for men, women and juniors are among the most prestigious. The World Championship finals start from

Figure skaters display their talent at Rondy on Ice. (Harry M. Walker)

downtown the last weekend of the festival and people line the streets watching the dogs run. The Fur Rondy championship is the first in a

LEFT: *David Terry (left) and Kim Williams urge their reindeer around the oval at Mulcahy Park during the World Championship Reindeer Race. (Harry M. Walker)*

BELOW LEFT: *A spinner shows off her skill at the arts and crafts show. (Harry M. Walker)*

BELOW: *Gian R. Cassarino, a former Disney artist, creates a character for the snow sculpture competition. (Harry M. Walker)*

triple-crown lineup of sled dog sprint races that includes the North American in Fairbanks and the Race of Champions in Tok.

The spirit of sports tournaments that formed the first Anchorage festival continues. Today's Fur Rondy has the All-Alaska Basketball Classic hosting as many as 10 teams from outside the city. The hockey competition between Fairbanks and Anchorage now occurs as part of an international hockey tournament hosted by the Anchorage Aces, a professional men's team in the West Coast Hockey League, which includes the Gold Kings of Fairbanks. The invitational tournament has brought teams to Anchorage from Norway, Russia, Canada and Japan.

Fur Rondy's steady growth through the years resulted in creation of Greater Anchorage Inc., a nonprofit organization set up specifically to manage the festival. Today, GAI produces about a dozen of the Fur Rondy events; the rest are sponsored by other groups, clubs and organizations as fund-raisers during an otherwise slow time of year.

Here are a few traditional Fur Rondy highlights:

• **Snowshoe softball** is a comical event to play and watch as teams try to bat and field while flailing around on snowshoes. Early versions of the game included swigging a shot of whiskey or beer for every base gained, but this practice is discouraged now.

• **Outhouse races** spoof what is still a "modern" convenience for many Alaskans. In this event, teams build outlandish portable potties to pull, push or peddle in competition.

• The **Wild Game Feed** is a free feast of Alaska venison, fish, fowl, even marine mammals such as whale and seal. People line up for blocks to file through Stewart's Photo downtown to fill their plates.

• The **Native Musicale**, a Rondy event for about 15 years, brings Native Alaska groups to West High School auditorium to perform spiritual and gospel music. Nearly a dozen Native groups from outside Anchorage perform, and the concert is broadcast to Bush communities.

• The **Eskimo blanket toss**, a standard event the last weekend of the festival for the last 25 years, is open to anyone who wants to try bouncing on the human-powered trampoline. The blanket toss originated with Eskimos who lived along the treeless coast and used a skin to bounce hunters into the sky. ●

BELOW: *There's something for everyone, even bowlers. (Harry M. Walker)*

RIGHT: *A participant in the Eskimo blanket toss gets a different view of the carnival area. (Harry M. Walker)*

A Young City Emerges

The 1950s found the still-small town of Anchorage struggling to cope with its tremendous population growth. The military continued to figure prominently in the economy as one of the biggest employers but its expanding presence put additional strains on the town. A critical shortage in housing, inadequate utility services, crowded schools, rampant vice and a serious lack of funds for improvements plagued Anchorage. A construction boom of military and federally funded public works projects, along with private investments, eased the crisis, allowing the town to reach an equilibrium of sorts. In the late '50s, Anchorage celebrated Alaska's statehood, as well as the territory's first big oil strike south of town on the Kenai Peninsula. These two events would considerably change Anchorage again, nudging it toward its modern identity.

By the early 1950s, Anchorage already had risen to an enviable status in the territory. Not only had it beaten out Valdez and Cordova for the railroad, Anchorage more recently had lured the District Court and other government agencies from Valdez and Juneau. Businessman Ralph Browne notes in a report on the city he wrote for the Alaska Development Board in 1952: "...discernible is

LEFT: *Road Closed and Detour signs typify the late summer scene in Anchorage when the ground thaws enough to allow road crews and contractors to repair the damage caused by spring breakup and the freeze-thaw cycles of the region's climate. This photo was taken looking east on Debarr Road approaching Russian Jack Springs Park. (Alaskana Photo-Art)*

FACING PAGE: *Town Square, the Alaska Center for the Performing Arts (left) and the William A. Egan Civic and Convention Center add elegance to downtown. (Harry M. Walker)*

a certain amount of not-too-well-concealed resentment harbored against the community. Such resentment is motivated by jealousy at the rapid and prosperous growth which Anchorage has experienced. Some would like nothing better than to see Anchorage fall on its economic face."

The military continued to play a major role in Anchorage during this decade. The start of the Cold War brought rapid military buildup throughout the territory as the United States armed itself, vowing to stop the spread of communism. Korea was aggressing against its neighbors and the Soviet Union had built up its forces in Siberia while perfecting nuclear capabilities. In 1954, the Soviets detonated an atomic bomb on Wrangel Island, in the Arctic

Ocean. Defense planners had already decided that Alaska would be the nation's first-line defense against Soviet bombers. Air-defense radar units were built, as was the Distant Early Warning System, a series of missile detection sites across the Arctic. The military also constructed White Alice communications sites. Anchorage became the headquarters for all of this.

In October 1950, a new Fort Richardson opened in the Chugach Mountain foothills about seven miles north of the original post. In 1947, the U.S. Air Force had been made a separate entity, and Anchorage's World War II installation with Elmendorf Field was turned over to the Air Force. Elmendorf became home to the newly created Alaskan Command and Alaskan Air Command. The military reservation was huge, encompassing present-day Campbell Tract, Russian Jack Springs and the Nunaka Valley residential area, so the Army simply moved to another section and rebuilt its post.

Anchorage, meanwhile, was trying to accommodate the influx of new people. Despite spending nearly $5 million after the war to improve the city's utilities and streets and another $1.6 million to build new schools, Anchorage's problems were as acute as ever. Property owners carried

This September 1954 view from the port of Anchorage shows the young city spread out toward the Chugach foothills. The tall building at center is the McKinley Apartment Building, known now as the MacKay Building; the large building at left was at that time a 400-bed tuberculosis sanatorium known as Alaska Native Services. In 1996 the building served as a general hospital, but a new Alaska Native hospital is under construction on Tudor Road and scheduled to open in 1997. In the foreground rests the Sacketts Harbor, a salvaged oil tanker with a 5,400-kilowatt generator that was beached at the port in 1946 to provide supplemental power for the growing city. (Steve McCutcheon Photo, courtesy of Anchorage Museum)

When temperatures are cold enough to create a solid covering of ice, residents near Westchester Lagoon clear off a makeshift rink for ice skating. The Union Oil building (with sign) and the taller ARCO towers provide the backdrop. (Danny Daniels)

the local tax burden for city improvements, incurring a single 85-percent jump in property taxes at one point. Despite repeated efforts, however, voters consistently rejected a sales tax.

According to Browne, Anchorage's "deficits" were in the areas of housing, schools, recreational facilities, juvenile delinquency, illicit activities, electrical power, domestic and industrial water supplies, sewage and garbage disposal, fire and police protection, streets and sidewalks, traffic and harbor improvements. In other words, almost everything.

"Anchorage's problems have received far more publicity than its assets," he wrote. "The city has been described as a boom-town, flash-in-the-pan, the longest-bar-in-the-world, and almost everything else to connote temporariness, instability, even immorality."

One of Anchorage's most pressing needs in the early 1950s was housing. Laborers, veterans and others moving to the prosperous frontier for jobs found few places to live. One conservative estimate at the time predicted a need for nearly 3,000 additional housing units every year through 1956 in Alaska, most of them in the Anchorage area. Several new apartment complexes built in the early 1950s began to meet the need, but in general most of the available housing was substandard. Tar-paper shacks, lean-tos and decrepit trailers constituted many of the living quarters in communities like Spenard outside the city limits, where there were no building codes. Even inside the city, 17 percent of the housing was considered substandard. Quonset and Pacific huts from Whittier and the Aleutians were brought to Government Hill for families of laborers working to rehabilitate the railroad, a $75-million project started in 1947.

Noted Browne, "It is true of Anchorage that a large number of persons live in trailers and there are a number of shacks and dives, but it also is true that such places are outnumbered substantially by fine, modern homes and large beautiful apartment buildings.

"Likewise, it is admitted there have been murders, narcotic arrests, armed robberies, sluggings, etc., but such evils are not uncommon to communities experiencing rapid growth accompanied by an overdose of prosperity. Less well-advertised…are the activities of the city's various social and cultural groups…. It is hardly fair to judge or label a community on a minority of conditions or actions of a few of its parasitic inhabitants."

The police department, however, was nothing to rave about during this time. Evangeline Atwood writes that seven police chiefs were ousted by 1956 for unprofessional behavior.

Anchorage in the 1950s was still tiny, geographically. The city didn't extend south much past the park strip, having annexed a 21-block area of mostly government housing called South Addition in 1945. Only 4th and 5th avenues downtown were paved. Spenard Road went southwest from downtown to Lake Spenard and on to the airport, and the two-laned Seward Highway went south eventually connecting to the road out of Seward. Northern Lights road was a far piece out of town. Lake Otis and Boniface roads to the east were gravel at best, and Tudor was still something to joke about. Someone even printed up bumper stickers that bragged "I drove Tudor Road,"

remembers Jack Roderick, who arrived in Anchorage in 1954 as a truck driver and soon became active in politics.

While the city itself was small, with only about 11,250 people in 1950, leapfrog development was claiming its outskirts. In 1950, some 18,800 people lived outside the city on homesteads and in the "suburbs" such as Spenard, Eastchester, Mountain View and Woodland Park. Within five years, the suburban population had jumped considerably. A new slogan took hold: "The fastest-growing little town under the Stars and Stripes." The growth occurred with no planning, and haphazard subdivisions sprang up, connected by an equally hap-hazard assortment of gravel roads and dirt trails. Traffic congestion became a problem, particularly on Spenard Road where stores and businesses were locating near the

FACING PAGE: *Campbell Lake is among the most upscale of Anchorage neighborhoods. (Steve McCutcheon)*

RIGHT: *Anchorage has a notable population of urban wildlife from moose and an occasional bear, to coyote, weasel, muskrat, seldom-seen lynx and other mammals. All animals need to be treated with respect, and it is best to view wild animals from afar. (Danny Daniels)*

Spenard Piggly Wiggly, which had opened in the late 1940s as Anchorage's first shopping center. The Anchorage City Transit Service, a subsidiary of Matanuska Valley Lines Inc., started running regular routes through the suburbs.

The Spenard community formed a public utility district to provide electrical power. Other neighborhoods received electricity from Chugach Electric Association, created through the Rural Electrification Administration. But homes and businesses outside the city lacked water and sewer hookups. As the population grew, the need for these services became critical.

People in some of the communities, like Spenard, discussed incorporating to have a tax base for services; others wanted the city to extend its water and sewer systems.

BELOW: *As the town developed and transportation improved, Anchorage became a collection point for furs that would be sent Outside to be sold. Pioneer furrier David Green opened a shop downtown in the 1950s; his sons still run the business. Perry Green, one of the sons, is a nationally renowned poker player. (Ernest Manewal)*

RIGHT: *Star, the pet reindeer of Oro Stewart and her late husband, Ivan, attracts passersby to the corner of 10th Avenue and I Street. (Penny Rennick)*

Annexation became one of Anchorage's big political issues. Although the city was having trouble providing services to the increasing population within its existing boundaries, annexation was seen by many as a better alternative than splitting the limited territorial and federal funds with new towns.

Not everyone wanted to be annexed, of course. Some resisted because they didn't want city services, or felt they couldn't afford the taxes; others associated with bars, strip joints and massage parlors didn't want to be under the city's jurisdiction. Likewise, it was the "upstanding" folks in the outlying areas who often agitated the most for annexation, hoping to run out their undesirable neighbors.

In 1954, four sections of Eastchester were annexed and the night after it was official, the bars closed early at 2 a.m., and one shut down completely because it had operated without a territorial license.

A slew of annexations followed: In 1958, Russian Jack Springs was deeded to the city by the military and annexed; Rogers Park, a 10-square-mile area with only about 450 people, voted to annex that year also. The last annexation of the decade occurred in 1959 with Spenard and most of Fairview, increasing the city's population to 37,000 and its area to 12.7 square miles.

As Anchorage leaders looked at where the city could expand, its options were limited by water to the west and the military reservation to the north, and the mountains to the east. Some people wanted to bridge Knik Arm with a road to open up land on the other side of the inlet. Swamps and muskeg lowlands on the south of town would require expensive draining and filling for construction. As it was, mosquitoes lived in the wetlands, which were sprayed with DDT pesticide.

In the meantime, Anchorage was becoming a distribution center with businesses offering mail-order services and area-wide deliveries. Completion of the highway to Seward and paving of the Glenn Highway to Palmer in 1954 gave trucking firms a wide area to service. Labor unions, bolstered by the military and civilian construction

The bluffs of Kincaid Park serve as a perfect launching site for paragliders. This glider sails over the algae-covered mud flats that fringe Anchorage's Cook Inlet shore. Lowlands of the Kenai Peninsula rise in the distance. (Alaskana Photo-Art)

boom, gained strength. Anchorage leaders renewed efforts to develop the port, to lower costs of getting materials into town. The railroad had promised repeatedly to improve the port, but cited winter icing conditions and the extreme tides as the reasons it hadn't. It also didn't want to lose rail freight to shipping companies, two of which had approached the city with interest. The city formed a port commission to look into the matter, and the U.S. Army Corps of Engineers launched a feasibility study.

Downtown, 4th Avenue was bustling, with stores and offices beginning to outnumber the bars. 5th Avenue had potential to become a main thoroughfare with the paving of the Glenn, and bold retailers dared to open stores there. One of the first was Wolf's Department Store at 5th and C streets.

Tourism expanded, with about 30,000 visitors flying and driving into town each year. The Junior Chamber of Commerce, a group of young business owners, opened a visitors' information center downtown in a log cabin on the city hall lawn. About this same time, the library moved out of city hall into a new building on 5th Avenue. It was built

Each summer fishermen head to the port area to try for the king salmon that run up Ship Creek. Since 1993, a king salmon derby has been held at Ship Creek. Proceeds from the derby benefit the Foster Grandparent/Senior Companion programs. (Alaskana Photo-Art)

with an endowment from the Loussac Foundation, established by Russian-born pioneer druggist, mine operator and realtor Z.J. Loussac to promote activities and education for Anchorage's youth.

The 1950s also brought television to Anchorage. Within four days of each other, KTVA and KTUU went on the air in 1953. Thousands of television sets were sold. Finally, Anchorage residents could see national news, sports and entertainment, albeit shows were delayed by hours and days, since the films had to be flown north for rebroadcast.

The last half of the 1950s were history-making years for Anchorage and Alaska. The push for statehood succeeded and the first oil strike occurred.

The campaign for statehood had played so well that in 1955 the territorial legislature funded a Constitutional Convention at the university in Fairbanks. Delegates from throughout Alaska, including Steve McCutcheon and others from Anchorage, met for 73 days and drafted a state constitution, to impress on federal lawmakers that Alaskans were ready to take on new responsibilities. A driving reason for statehood was to outlaw fish traps being used by the canneries and destroying the salmon runs. Alaska voters overwhelmingly ratified their new constitution in 1956. Now it was up to Congress.

Also that year, Anchorage basked in the honor of being named an "All-American City," proudly proclaiming the distinction with a banner over 4th Avenue. Award sponsors Look Magazine and the National Municipal League recognized Anchorage for "successfully tackling a skyrocketing population that threatened to swamp city facilities and pushing for needed civic improvements," according to *Anchorage, Star of the North.*

Then in 1957, Richfield Oil Co. (later Atlantic Richfield) announced its discovery of oil in the federal moose range on the Kenai Peninsula. It was to be a boon for the city of Anchorage, as well as a windfall for some of its most prominent residents; the company's strikes were on leases obtained from Atwood and his business partners, who'd bought up tracts on informed speculation.

The territory lobbied the federal government to open the moose range to drilling, which was quickly accomplished with little challenge. With millions of dollars at stake, oil suddenly became big business in Anchorage. Although towns on the Kenai courted the company representatives, Anchorage became their choice for operation headquarters. More than a dozen companies opened offices in Anchorage

Chugach State Park is a perfect backyard for Anchorage. The 495,204-acre park offers abundant hiking, diverse wildlife and outstanding views of the city. The Glen Alps and Prospect Heights residential areas of the Hillside provide good access to the park. Here Chuck Kennedy relaxes on top of The Ramp, 5,240 feet, overlooking Ship Lake. (Jon R. Nickles)

LEFT: *The statehood monument at the foot of E Street overlooking Ship Creek and the Port of Anchorage commemorates Alaska's entrance into the union as the 49th state in 1959 during the Eisenhower presidency. (George Wuerthner)*

BELOW LEFT: *Newest addition to the University of Alaska Anchorage campus is the Business Education Building, opened in 1993 and built at a cost of $22.6 million. (Alaskana Photo-Art)*

FACING PAGE: *Visitor central for downtown Anchorage is the corner of 4th Avenue and F Street. Pioneer industrialist Austin (Cap) Lathrop built the 4th Avenue Theater, which opened in the 1940s. (George Wuerthner)*

as they launched exploration operations on the Kenai and in Cook Inlet. The west side of Cook Inlet would prove lucrative for developers, but the Kenai was another matter. Although dozens of leases would be drilled on land, the Swanson River site originally struck by Richfield would be the only producing Kenai field.

Perhaps the discovery of oil made Alaska more valuable as a state, or perhaps the territory's clamoring residents had finally made their point, but on June 30, 1958, the U.S. Senate voted to admit Alaska to the Union. At the *Times,* Atwood cranked up the presses for a special edition. "WE'RE IN" shouted the 7-inch-high banner headline. Townspeople gathered on the park strip to celebrate with a giant bonfire, burning 50 tons of lumber, a ton for each state, Alaska and Hawaii. Alaskans voted 5-to-1 that August to accept statehood; the vote in Anchorage was 18-to-1. Alaska was given entitlement to select 103.5 million acres from federal land holdings, along with $28.5 million to set up its new state government. Anchorage would become the administrative center, and Atwood would soon launch an editorial campaign to remove the state capital from Juneau. ∎

Earthquakes
and Oil

The heady rush of statehood and oil exploration carried Anchorage into the 1960s. Almost overnight, Anchorage had become the largest city in the newest state. The most solid of institutions — the federal railroad and the military — anchored its economy, and now its downtown droned with oilmen chaperoning a $30-million investment in the region. A sense of permanence prevailed. Opportunities seemed limitless, particularly with momentum building to relocate the state capital near Anchorage, and the town's rapid growth continued.

The decade of the 60s, however, was most vividly marked by two events that commanded national attention. The Good Friday earthquake of 1964 ravaged southcentral Alaska, killing 115 people, displacing hundreds more, and doing millions of dollars in property damage. It was the most powerful quake to hit North America this century. Nine people died in Anchorage during the quake, an amazingly few considering the city's large population and the extent of destruction. Again, the federal government came to Anchorage's aid and within months, the recovering city was undergoing something of an economic flush as people started rebuilding.

The second historical marker occurred in 1968, with discovery of the Prudhoe Bay oil field on the North Slope. Anchorage swarmed with oilmen and speculators positioning themselves to grab part of the action. The state held a lease sale for North Slope oil in downtown Anchorage, and more than $900 million came across the table in sealed bids.

LEFT: *Much of the land south of the original townsite of Anchorage was wetland, which has been filled in as the town has grown. Creeks that laced the area have been rechanneled to allow drainage for building sites. (Pete K. Martin)*

FACING PAGE: *A fog bank hangs low over south Anchorage in this view of traffic heading south on Minnesota Drive. (Danny Daniels)*

A bustling city lines the Knik Arm shore in this August 1963 view. At lower left Gambell Street curves across Chester Creek flats and into downtown Anchorage. The baseball diamond at Mulcahy Park is visible, as is the expansion of the Anchorage Westward Hotel and the yellow Hill Building. (Pete K. Martin)

When the oil companies announced plans to build a pipeline across Alaska to carry oil to tankers in Valdez, Anchorage braced for another boom.

But all that was still ahead when the decade started. Anchorage still felt like a small town, say people who lived here then. People were friendly, willing to help each other and most everyone knew everyone else — or so it seemed. It probably was not all that close-knit, given the population figures and the rapid in-migration of new-comers, but it was still small geographically.

By 1960, 82,833 people lived in the Anchorage area; 44,237 of them inside the city. Each year brought close to 4,000 additional people into the area, and by 1965 the Anchorage bowl held more than 102,000 residents. By the end of the decade, that number would climb to 126,385. Anchorage was like a magnet, drawing people and industry and money. Its modern economic identity was beginning to gel with state and federal government, the military, oil and tourism.

The Swanson River oil field on the Kenai swung into full production with 52 wells by 1961, supporting construction of a refinery at Nikiski. A pipeline from Kenai under Cook Inlet into Anchorage allowed townspeople to hook up to natural gas for heating and cooking, a cheaper alternative to electricity. Oil exploration and development moved to the west side of Cook Inlet and in 1963, Shell Oil Co. announced its first strike. Soon oil drilling platforms dotted the horizon, their lights sometimes visible across the inlet at night.

It was a decade of building landmarks. In 1960, Alaska Methodist University, the city's first four-year college, opened its doors. Located in the forest east of town, its centerpiece was a three-building student union-dorm complex, designed by architect Edward Durell Stone who also designed the Kennedy Center in Washington, D.C. Today, this complex is known as Atwood Hall, named to honor Evangeline and Robert Atwood who helped fund repairs and renovations.

Closer in, the Northern Lights Shopping Center at the corner of Northern Lights Boulevard and Spenard Road opened for business. Anchoring the new shopping center was Caribou Department Store, which later merged with Montgomery Wards and was known for many years as Caribou-Wards. It was one of the places in town to shop,

along with the new J.C. Penney store and the Northern Commercial Co. downtown. Today, REI occupies the Caribou-Wards building.

The center's developer, Walter Hickel, had built 88 apartments and houses downtown after the war in separate partnerships with Emil Pfeil and Karl Martin. To take in Anchorage's increasing numbers of tourists and business travelers, he built the Traveler's Inn on Gambell Street at the site of a former mink farm, and another hotel by the same name in Fairbanks. In the 1950s he and World War II veteran Col. Marvin "Muktuk" Marston had developed

Thirty years ago, the Muldoon area presented a natural landscape; it is all built up today. (Pete K. Martin)

a residential area southwest of downtown overlooking the inlet. Popularly known as Turnagain-by-the Sea, it had become the home-building location of choice for many of Anchorage's leading citizens.

Elsewhere in town, the Lathrop Co. carried on the empire-building vision of its late founder Austin E. Lathrop. This wealthy industrialist had built the Empress Theater downtown in 1915 and completed the art deco 4th Avenue Theater in 1947, three years before his death. In the 1960s, the Lathrop Co. let loose a flurry of construction projects including the downtown Hill Building, the Denali Theater on Spenard, the Fireweed Theater and Sundowner Drive-In at the corner of Fireweed and the Seward Highway.

Downtown, newspaper publisher Atwood and his partners in the Westward Hotel decided to build a high-rise addition. Atwood also cranked up his editorial campaign promoting the capital move. Voters statewide rejected the idea in 1960 and 1962; Alaskans outside the railbelt, particularly in Southeast, didn't want Anchorage or Fairbanks, the state's two largest towns, to end up being the seat of government too. But with Atwood's persistence, the subject was destined to reappear.

The earthquake in 1964 interrupted everything. Politics, commerce, life as usual throughout Southcentral Alaska stopped and for a terrifying matter of moments, survival was all that mattered. Kristin Domela, 7-years-old at the time, rode out the quake with her mother and brother in their home in Turnagain, one of the five areas in Anchorage where major landslides occurred.

Kristin remembers hanging onto the living room couch and looking out the front window. One second, she saw a neighbor's house in the distance. The next second, she saw nothing but dirt pressing against the window. Her home was tilting. Kristin's mother led her and her brother up the now-steeply inclining hall to the bathroom where they climbed up into the tub. When the shaking stopped, the silence was deafening, she said. Then the shouting and crying started, the sounds of people in the neighborhood calling for help. The Domela trio climbed out through the

LEFT: *This pastoral scene of Baxter Lake and birch and spruce forest taken in 1969 no longer exists. The lake is now virtually surrounded by single and multifamily housing. (Pete K. Martin)*

FACING PAGE: *Only a few businesses seen today along 5th Avenue looking west are recognizable in this summer 1963 photo. The J.C. Penney department store, the large building at left, opened in 1963. The earthquake the following year severely damaged the building, which was quickly repaired so the store could reopen. (Pete K. Martin)*

This view shows downtown Anchorage as it appeared looking southeast from the J.C. Penney parking garage in 1967. The closest street is D. The red building facing D Street is now an art gallery; the area across D from the building is now parking lot. (Pete K. Martin)

federal government, national relief agencies and concerned individuals. People grieved for lost family and friends, and tried to help each other as best they could. In Anchorage, victims salvaged what they could to start over as the city tried to restore electrical power, water and sewer, clear debris and reopen roads. Health agencies launched a typhoid immunization program, out of concern for contaminated food and water. The military organized manpower, equipment and airlifts to meet needs of the distressed state, and in Anchorage their help included helicopter rescues, food kitchens and patrols to prevent vandalism and looting. The Federal Reconstruction Commission coordinated federal funding for recovery, an amount between $325 and $414 million (1964 dollars) for highways, public works, urban renewal, and mortgage relief to business and home owners whose properties had been destroyed or damaged.

Most people in Anchorage simply wanted life to return to normal as soon as possible. Rebuilding started almost immediately. At the same time, a task force of scientists, engineers and geologists offered a series of recommendations about reconstruction, based on their assessments of ground instability, but few of their ideas were followed. For instance, they advised moving downtown away from the west bluffs along L Street, where the ground had cracked and started moving and could collapse in a future great quake. Nothing came of this suggestion, resisted by private landowners with sizable investments in the area. Within months, Wally Hickel broke ground for his Captain Cook Hotel just east of the slide; he said he wanted to show confidence in downtown. A year after the quake, the city assembly rezoned the L Street slide area to permit higher residential density and to allow office use and high-rise construction.

The only area of downtown stabilized in accordance with the task force recommendations was along 4th Avenue, where the ground had collapsed. Most of the property belonged to the federal railroad and was easily acquired for urban renewal.

bathroom window and started heading up the collapsed slope toward safer ground. Trying to pick their way over huge chunks of earth and around deep chasms in the ground was terrifying. "The earth is supposed to be like a mother, and it opens up and swallows everything. It leaves you with a different concept of life," Kristin said recently from her home in Girdwood. The ground where their home stood is now part of Earthquake Park.

In the days, weeks and months following the earthquake, Alaskans received a massive outpouring of help from the

In Turnagain, nearly $684,000 was spent in stabilization studies. The Army Corps of Engineers concluded that the slide zone was essentially stable landward of the slide, which formed a natural buttress, if the buttress was protected against beach erosion. The Alaska State Housing Authority recommended that the slide area not be rebuilt but acquired for use as a park, with erosion control and a road along the waterfront. Although the western end of the Turnagain slide area was made into Earthquake Park, the assembly voted in 1967 to consider building applications in the remaining part. After years of discussion and legalities, property owners are now being allowed to rebuild there. For more about the earthquake, please see page 80.

In the building boom that followed the quake, mid-town Anchorage took on much of its current look. Sub-divisions platted in the late '50s and early '60s, including Windemere at the west end of Tudor Road and College

FACING PAGE: *The Resolution Plaza building overlooks Ship Creek and the port and was designed with state-of-the-art construction because the area is susceptible to sloughing during strong earthquakes. (Harry M. Walker)*

RIGHT: *You're never too young to take up one of Alaska's favorite pastimes, as these youngsters at Goose Lake prove. (Harry M. Walker)*

Village, east of the Seward Highway off Northern Lights. Grocer Larry Carr and his partner, Barney Gottstein, announced plans in 1966 for the Anchorage Shopping Center, billed as Alaska's largest shopping complex, next to the new Sears store on Northern Lights. An enclosed mall with a modern Alaskana theme would connect the Sears store with Carrs food market and liquor store and include 30 other shops. Two years later, the Aurora Village shopping center with another Carrs market was built on west Northern Lights. Larry Carr had opened his first grocery in the early 1950s, in a Quonset hut at the edge of town on the corner of 13th and Gambell. Here shoppers could buy fresh meat, fruits and vegetables, flown in three times a week from Outside by special charters that Carr arranged.

Downtown, the skyline was rising. Along with the Captain Cook Hotel, the 9-story First National Bank went up. The J.C. Penney store was rebuilt in the same location, this time with a high-rise attached parking garage. The Westward Hotel quickly reopened after repairs to minor structural damage, and soon boasted the second parking garage in downtown.

Anchorage's cultural scene rebounded just as quickly. Performing groups and organizations included the Civic Ballet under direction of ballerina Lynda Lorimer Kaiser, the Anchorage Lyric Opera Theater, the Anchorage Concert Association, the Anchorage Community Chorus, the Alaska Artists Guild, the Philharmonic Orchestra, and the Anchorage Community Theater led by Frank Brink in

a Quonset hut near the intersection of Minnesota Drive and Northern Lights Boulevard.

About this time, two local grocers won a 300-pound elephant from India in a national sales contest. To keep the elephant, they rented heated stall space from Sammye Seawell at the Diamond H Riding Academy. With money raised by school children, the Alaska Zoo was built in the country on the far east edge of town, and opened in 1969 with Annabelle the elephant, two black bear cubs, an arctic fox and a baby harbor seal.

Two years after the earthquake, Anchorage celebrated its second All-American City designation. Valdez and Seward also shared the 1966 honor, bestowed on the cities in a joint ceremony in Anchorage. The next year, Anchorage joined other cities throughout the state in the centennial

celebration commemorating the purchase of Alaska from Russia 100 years earlier. Just as surely, the centennial gave communities a celebratory focus for the post-quake recovery. The centennial was also the occasion for funding construction of the city's first museum at 7th Avenue and A Street.

That year also saw a change in Alaska's political landscape. Anchorage's hotel owner and developer Walter Hickel was elected governor, succeeding Gov. William Egan who had held the post since statehood. Anchorage attorney Howard Pollock won the state's lone Congressional seat in that election, upsetting incumbent Rep. Ralph Rivers. Hickel and Pollock were the first Republicans to hold these offices, and, for the first time, the state legislature had a Republican majority. Up to that time in state politics, Anchorage had played "a loveless role," wrote Evangeline Atwood in *Anchorage, Star of the North.* "It was generally viewed as a brash up-start bent on expanding economically at the expense of the rest of the state." Now, for the first time, Anchorage had political clout. This was amplified two years later when Anchorage realtor Mike Gravel ousted incumbent Ernest Gruening from the U.S. Senate, and Gov. Hickel appointed Anchorage attorney and state Rep. Ted Stevens to fill the other U.S. Senate seat, left open by the death of E.L. "Bob" Barlett.

The announcement in 1968 by Atlantic Richfield and Humble Oil of a giant oil strike at Prudhoe Bay on Alaska's North Slope electrified Anchorage, as well as the rest of the state and nation. With recoverable reserves estimated at the time to be five to 10 million barrels of oils, Prudhoe Bay was one of the largest oil fields in the world.

The significance of the find became apparent to any who

Eagle River, just east of Anchorage, challenges white-water enthusiasts. The river begins at Eagle Glacier in the Chugach Mountains and flows 40 miles to enter Knik Arm nine miles northeast of Anchorage. (Alaskana Photo-Art)

doubted when the state held its next North Slope lease sale. These sales had been held twice a year in Anchorage since 1964, but had rarely drawn much attention or interest. But the September 10, 1969, sale proved entirely different. As Evangeline Atwood wrote: "Hotel rooms were booked solid for days before the sale as petroleum executives arrived. Newspaper, radio and television personnel from as far as London were on the scene. Wire photo lines and teletype were laid into Sydney Laurence Auditorium to help record the event." Oilmen who couldn't find rooms slept in their corporate jets, if they weren't going over last-minute calculations of final bids with their bankers. On the morning of the sale in the auditorium heavily guarded by state police, oil representatives submitted 1,105 individually sealed bids totaling more than $900 million.

As the largest city in the new oil state, Anchorage's role as corporate oil headquarters would expand. The city's powerful and vocal pro-development contingent would be challenged and questioned in ways never before seen or heard. Oil industry plans to build a pipeline across Alaska, from the North Slope to tidewater at Valdez, opened Anchorage to another boom, as people moved in and businesses geared up for pipeline construction.

"That (oil) discovery...set in motion an extraordinary drama, which has pitted those who prefer the more traditional Alaska way of life against those who favor full-scale development of the state's resources — with most Alaskans falling somewhere in between," wrote Peter Gruenstein and John Hanrahan in *The Lost Frontier* (1977). ■

LEFT: *Tripods with panels of historical information guide visitors along a walking tour in downtown Anchorage. (Harry M. Walker)*

FACING PAGE: *Bowhead and beluga whales course the blue waters of the Wayland Wall, named for the artist who painted the scene on the west wall of the J.C. Penney store. (Penny Rennick)*

The Good Friday Earthquake

By L.J. Campbell

On March 27, 1964, Anchorage experienced one of the most powerful earthquakes on record. Giant rock slabs grinding past each other deep beneath the floor of Prince William Sound, at the head of College Fjord about 80 miles east of Anchorage, wrenched apart at 5:36 p.m. that day. The massive tear released a surge of shock waves felt over more than 700,000 square miles. It was the strongest earthquake to hit North America this century.

Southcentral Alaska suffered the brunt of the quake and shook violently in savage pulses for three to four minutes and perhaps as long as seven minutes in some places. Witnesses in downtown Anchorage reported asphalt streets rippling with waves 5 feet high. Cars bounced around as if on a trampoline, chimneys fell and many buildings rocked off their foundations, some collapsing. Giant cracks in the ground opened and closed, spewing geysers of water and sand. Five major landslides wrecked much of the city, the most horrific taking blocks of homes in Turnagain on the bluffs overlooking Cook Inlet, southwest of downtown. Land here churned like a mangled jigsaw puzzle, and homes broke apart, sliding toward the water as the ground beneath them collapsed.

In Anchorage, the damage was most severe

Many homes were lost and some residents died in the Turnagain area. The parents of the two Mead children who died in the earthquake donated their property to the city in 1980. The site is now Telequana Park. (Steve McCutcheon)

in areas underlain by a water-saturated clay. This Bootlegger's Cove clay, as it is known, changed consistency because of the severity and duration of the shaking, turning jellylike and in the worst cases, liquefying and flowing downhill, collapsing the surface into craters and causing landslides.

The quake wrought devastation all along Alaska's coast, and the communities of Valdez and Seward were particularly hard hit with death and destruction from underwater landslides that splashed harbor waves called seiches back into town. Sea waves, or tsunamis, obliterated Chenega and several villages on Kodiak Island, including much of Kodiak town. Dozens of people died in Valdez and Chenega, and the communities were so completely destroyed that both were subsequently rebuilt at different locations.

All told, the quake killed 115 people in Alaska, nine of whom died in Anchorage. Another 15 people died along the coasts of Oregon and California from tsunamis. The earthquake did more than $300 million (in 1964 dollars) in property damage in Alaska, about $86 million of which occurred in Anchorage. The destruction of vital port facilities at Whittier and Seward and bridges, railroad track and roadways paralyzed the state's commerce for a time.

With a power 10 times greater than the atomic bomb that leveled Hiroshima, the '64 Alaska quake reached far and wide. Ground vibrations were felt throughout Alaska, from Barrow to Sitka. It dramatically rearranged the land throughout southern Alaska along an arch about 600 miles long that generally paralleled the Gulf of Alaska coastline. A swath of land some 250 miles wide was measurably displaced, with the area northwest and landward of this line dropping an average of 2.5 feet and up to 7.5 feet. The area southeast and seaward of the line rose an average of 6 feet. In specific locations, including the landslide areas in Anchorage, the deformation was even more drastic. In Prince William Sound, parts of Montague Island lifted 38 feet. The

quake generated tsunamis from the Gulf of Mexico to Antarctica. Undulations from the quake rippled the surface of North America, moving the ground two inches, and sloshed water in wells in South America.

The 1964 Alaska quake remains one of the most thoroughly studied earthquakes in history, with volumes of government reports devoted to it. In recent years, it was upgraded in magnitude from 8.4 to 9.2. Its devastation—certainly tremendous to those who lost lives and property—could have been many times worse had the region not been so sparsely populated. The fact that the earthquake occurred on a holiday, when schools and many offices were closed, and near the end of the business day when most people were headed home, spared the city of Anchorage from much greater tragedy. The

city fortunately escaped tsunamis, and an electrical power outage prevented explosions and fires from leaking gas lines. Broken water mains and clogged streets would have made fire fighting extremely difficult.

Anyone who lived through Alaska's Good Friday earthquake has an amazing story to tell. Here's a brief look at what happened in Anchorage during and after the great event, drawn from recent interviews with some of the people who experienced it, as well as newspaper accounts, magazine articles and books. These include National Academy of Sciences reports published in 1972 and a series in the *Anchorage Daily News* on the earthquake's 25th anniversary.

Anchorage on the Day of the Quake

Snow spit from the gray sky all that day throughout the Anchorage bowl, where about 94,500 people lived from Girdwood to Eagle River. Only about 50,000 of them lived within the actual city limits, a much smaller area that extended not as far south as Tudor Road and not as far east as Boniface Parkway. The city's central business district occupied downtown, at the head of a slope overlooking Knik Arm to the west and the Ship Creek flats to the north. Across the flats rose the steep bluffs up to Government Hill, one of the city's older residential areas with a school. With half the state's population, two major military bases located nearby, a large airport, port facilities, and home to numerous state and federal government agencies, Anchorage served as Alaska's nerve center.

Falling slabs from the newly opened J.C. Penney department store pulverized the sidewalk and crushed this car. Two people were killed by the falling concrete. (Steve McCutcheon)

Expansion of the Westward Hotel (now called the Anchorage Hilton Hotel) at 3rd Avenue and C Street towers over this view of 4th Avenue looking west in September 1963. Much of the right side of the block between C and D streets crumbled in the earthquake. (Pete K. Martin)

But on this Good Friday, the city was moving at a somewhat slower pace with schools and many offices closed for the holiday. The 4th Avenue Theater, one of two theaters downtown, was showing a new Disney movie and had seated about 700 vacationing youngsters for the afternoon matinee. A block over at 5th Avenue and D Street, the new J.C. Penney store was doing a brisk business. It was the city's first big department store, an impressive affair at five stories tall and covered on the outside with decorative concrete slabs almost the height of the building. It offered quite the shopping experience for the young, growing town. Children rode the escalators and watched the new televisions in the electronics department, while their parents browsed glass showcases of gift items, jewelry, crystal and china and tried on shoes and clothing.

In Turnagain, car salesman J.D. Peters was home recovering from the flu, awaiting his wife's return from work. Turnagain was the city's newest, swankiest residential area with a fringe of expensive custom homes. Developed by World War II veteran Marvin "Muktuk" Marston and Walter Hickel, the subdivision stretched along the bluffs overlooking Cook Inlet and offered spectacular views of the mountains across the water. Many of the town's more influential, wealthy residents lived in Turnagain on the coveted "view" lots close to the bluff's edge. The sites were not without drawbacks; at least one homeowner had complained that chunks of his yard were falling off the bluff.

Peters' neighbors included the town's only neurosurgeon, Dr. Perry Mead, and Robert Atwood, owner and publisher of the *Anchorage Daily Times* and a part-owner in the Westward Hotel. Atwood had just arrived home from work, as his wife left for a quick run to the grocery to pick up something for dinner. He got out his trumpet to practice a bit while the house was empty.

At the Hillside Apartments, on West 16th Avenue off I Street, Robert Girt was ironing a pair of pants, getting ready for a date with the girl down the hall. He was home on leave, having just completed a tour of duty in Korea. A younger brother and sister had been in and out all day, and his father, a nightclub entertainer, hadn't left for work. His mother, a cocktail waitress, had already gone to her job at the Fourth Avenue bar.

At the All Saints Episcopal Church downtown, worshippers had gathered for the Good Friday service. They listened as the Rev. Norm Elliot read from the Book of Matthew: "...Jesus cried with a loud voice and gave up his spirit. And behold, the curtain of the temple was torn in two from top to bottom, and the earth quaked, and the rocks were rent."

It was just past 5:30 p.m.

Forces At Play Under The Earth

Alaskans, generally, have a cavalier attitude about earthquakes. Almost anyone who has lived here for any time has experienced the sharp jolt, a momentary shake, of a temblor. The sensation is often mistaken for a large truck driving by. Dozens of small quakes, registering very minor to light in magnitude and only occasionally moderate to strong, are recorded each day by seismograph stations around the state. More than half the earthquakes that occur in the United States originate under Alaska, and 75 percent of those in Alaska occur in the Anchorage, Cook Inlet, Alaska Peninsula and Aleutian areas.

Alaska is one of the most active seismic regions of the world by virtue of its location. It sits near the boundary of two giant slabs of rock — the North American plate and the Pacific plate. In addition, its land mass is composed of many smaller rock slabs, or terranes, that collided from far distant sources millions of years ago when the continents were first forming. The juncture of these terranes and plates are called faults, and the greatest of the Alaska faults is where the Pacific and North American plates meet, a line that runs from the Queen Charlotte Islands of British Columbia along the southern coast of Alaska through the Aleutian Islands. It is at these fault lines that earthquakes originate, as the terranes and plates shift and move past, over and under each other in a continuation of geologic earth-building processes.

The Pacific plate moves northwestward in relation to the continental plate at a rate of about two inches a year, thrusting under the continent. These plates rarely glide past each other smoothly. Instead, rocks in various sections along the fault periodically snag against each other. Yet the thrusting force continues, accumulating at these sticking points. Often the snags dislodge rather quickly in a burp of motion hardly felt at the surface. But other snags can lock up for centuries, storing megatons of power. At some point, the tension becomes too great and the fault ruptures. The rocks break free, releasing a flood of pent-up energy that shoots to the surface with considerable disturbance.

In 1964, one such snag was located along the continental fault line, some 15 to 30 miles below Prince William Sound between Anchorage and Valdez. For perhaps 1,000 years, the movement of the plates had been locked here. Monumental pressure had been building. At a few seconds past 5:36 p.m., the rocks finally exploded with a fury. In one motion, the Pacific plate shot an estimated 65 feet laterally under the continental plate, ripping the earth along the fault line practically to the southern tip of Kodiak Island, some 125 miles from the epicenter. Shock waves pulsed through land and sea, like a savage beast clawing to escape through a tiny hole.

Impact

For the first few seconds, the vibrations seemed what Alaskans had come to accept as normal. "It started as sort of a rumble. We'd gone through shakers before, and it wasn't anything to get too upset about," recalls Robert Girt, who at age 50 still lives in Anchorage. He remembers looking up at some fancy glass wine carafes filled with colored water on a window sill in his family's apartment, thinking that if they fell off, they'd make a mess.

It quickly became obvious to Girt and everyone else in Southcentral Alaska that this was not a regular earthquake. The vibrations didn't die away, but grew stronger and increasingly violent.

Geologist John R. Williams, also in the

The quake demolished newspaper publisher Robert Atwood's home in the Turnagain area. Atwood also lost his trumpet when a crevasse opened and the publisher and his trumpet tumbled in. (Steve McCutcheon)

Hillside Apartment building at the time, later described the experience in a government report. He said the initial shaking of about 10 seconds was immediately followed by strong east-west rolling motions. As plaster fell in his apartment, he led his son into the outside hall, where they watched the exit door to the street twist out of square, breaking the glass. The glass blocks around the entrance started shattering. Concrete blocks in the walls were grating against each other. The pair ran outside and saw the building swaying and coming apart. The ground was heaving, and trees and utility poles were whipping and bending, in some cases touching the ground. Some people reported that the rolling motion shifted north and south a minute or so into the quake. Others described being knocked off their feet by vertical jolts. The most intense shock waves apparently lasted two to three minutes although

Soldiers patrolled the streets to direct traffic and prevent looting. (Steve McCutcheon)

some reports say the shaking was felt for as long as seven minutes.

As Girt groped to find something to hold onto, his brother dashed out of the apartment. Girt recalls he had trouble staying on his feet, the building was shaking, pitching and swaying so violently. "I knew it was time to get the hell out," he said. He and his father grabbed his little sister and headed downstairs to building's exit. Once they were safely out, he ran back inside to see about his neighbors. He attributes his calm demeanor at the time to military training. On the fourth floor landing, he found his girlfriend's mother, hugging the stair banister, too scared to move. Girt grabbed her by the hand, pulling her outside. Still the shaking continued, and the apartment building, built into the 16th Avenue bluff, was beginning to fail on its south side where three floors were supported by an underground parking garage. The neighbor said her elderly father, an invalid, was still inside, so Girt and his father returned to get him. As the smell of natural gas begin filling the air, Girt re-entered the building three more times to rescue other neighbors and finally his sister's cat.

On 4th Avenue, Girt's mother was serving two-for-one Happy Hour drinks when the bottles behind the bar started clattering and tables started dancing. Everyone headed for the front door, some patrons gripping a drink in each hand. As people poured onto 4th Avenue from businesses along the street, sections of downtown started sliding. Beneath the bar and its storefront neighbors between B and D streets, the ground separated in a yawning crevasse 100 to 150 feet wide and 11 feet deep. Buildings and sidewalks buckled and sank. People on the street linked arms to stay on their feet in case another crevasse opened. A lawyer rushed out of an athletic club where he'd been taking a steam and joined the wildly weaving human chain. No one seemed to notice that he was naked. At the 4th Avenue Theater, the manager sternly ordered children to stay in their seats and hold on, which they did for the most part; that building suffered little damage although the Denali Theater down the street sank into the crater.

Newspaper editor William Tobin had just parked his car in front of J.C. Penney when the quake hit. According to various published accounts, he felt his car lurch forward, and assumed he'd been rammed by a bad driver. As he saw that the car behind him was empty, his car started rocking side to side, as were other cars on the street. He noticed a woman in the street lurching back and forth, as if she was having a seizure. He jumped out of his car to help. As he and the woman held on to each other, he saw the street roll toward them in waves so tall he could not see over them. People on the street were hanging onto parking meters, which were rocking side to side.

Screeching, tearing sounds filled the air from the wrenching and twisting of wood, steel and mortar in the buildings. The decorative facade on the outside of J.C. Penney started breaking loose. Like a concrete curtain, the slabs crashed to the ground, crushing parked cars and all else in their path.

Inside Penney's, people were beginning to panic. Things started breaking apart. Up on the third floor, Air Force staff sergeant Roderick Howells and his wife were looking at bolts of cloth in the sewing department. As the tremors built, he ran toward his two children, who'd been watching television in the electronics department. Suddenly the floor dropped away.

He caught himself on the edge of the hole and started climbing up when a piece of ceiling slammed down, hitting him on the back. He shook it off and found his children as a second wave of shaking started. Mrs. Howells, meantime, was crawling toward her husband. The lights went off and in the darkness, amid the screams and shouts of the others, she followed the sound of his voice yelling to her that he'd found the children. When she reached him, they escaped down a back stairway and cleared the collapsing building in what they later called a miracle.

At the All Saints Episcopal Church, the words of Matthew still hung in the air when the sanctuary started moving. The chandeliers started swaying, then swinging back and forth, all the way up to hit the ceiling and return. The congregation rushed to the altar around the Rev. Elliot. At home in Turnagain, the pastor's wife Stella tried to hold onto her three children, an infant son and her 4- and 6-year-old daughters. Her 4-year-old darted away out the front door, and Stella ran after her, grabbing the child by the nape of her neck, just as the chimney fell off the house and crashed directly onto the spot where the girl had been headed. With the girls grabbing her legs and cradling her son, the foursome clung together as the ground around them rolled and the earth emitted a deafening roar.

To the west several blocks along the length of their subdivision, the earth was cracking apart as the bluffs pulled away, twisting and heaving and sliding toward Cook Inlet. Newspaper publisher Atwood ran outside as the inside of his writhing house started crashing down. In an account widely published afterwards, he described table-sized blocks of

ground pushing up like big toadstools as crevasses opened all around. He watched as a nearby house slid off its foundation toward the water. He tried to climb over the neighbor's fence, but the fence dropped away beneath him. He fell into a crevasse, his fall cushioned by a bed of sand. With his right arm embedded to the elbow in the sand, he couldn't move and watched in horror as another house started sliding into the crevasse with him. Pelted by debris including mailboxes and tree limbs, he struggled to free himself, realizing he was still gripping his trumpet buried in the sand beneath him. Letting go, he pulled himself free and climbed out.

The shaking likewise had rousted flu-ridden Peters from his house in time to see his wife returning in the car, starting to pull into the driveway. She stopped and got out and as he yelled to her, a crevasse opened between them. Before they

could find a way across, the ground shifted in another direction and the house reared up and began sliding toward the water of Cook Inlet. Peters yelled at his wife to hold on. Just as suddenly as it had appeared, the crevasse between them closed, tilting the ground under Mrs. Peters, sending her sliding toward her husband.

Aftermath

The shaking, rolling and sliding stopped finally in a passage of minutes that seemed an eternity. The town was in chaos as people sorted out what had happened. The lights were off, water mains and gas lines were broken, many streets impassable. Families were frantic to find their loved ones. Firemen and police started search and rescue efforts almost immediately,

Mac's Foto was just one of the businesses taken out when the north side of 4th Avenue sank. When the shaking was over, many Alaskans called on their sense of humor. Proprietor of Mac's Foto, Steve McCutcheon, a life-long Alaskan from a pioneer family, advised customers with his sign: "Closed due to Early Breakup." (William Wakeland, courtesy of Steve McCutcheon)

and various individuals throughout the city in official and unofficial capacity launched their own efforts to help their neighbors and assess

After the quake, Mac's Foto moved to a new location in the former McCutcheon family home on 7th just west of C Street. The occasion called for a new sign: "Business as usual (more or less) in spite of early breakup." (Steve McCutcheon)

the damage. But hours passed before emergency relief efforts were coordinated. Finally on Saturday morning at 3 a.m., city officials met with representatives from Red Cross, Salvation Army, the military and other agencies to organize the massive effort that would be required to get through the first days after the disaster.

The death toll was feared high in the initial hours after the quake. Some of the first news reports estimated as many as 600 had been

killed throughout Alaska, with hundreds dead in Anchorage.

In Anchorage, rescuers using mountain-climbing equipment searched the destroyed section of Turnagain Heights, where 75 homes slid away and another 145 homes were severely damaged. A length of bluff some 8,600 feet long had collapsed in a concave pattern that reached 600 feet into the subdivision at the east end and about twice that far on the west end. The ground cracked another 2,200 feet inland. Some of the houses ended up 35 feet below where they had originally sat.

Three people died in Turnagain. Mrs. Virgil Knight was crushed to death when her home collapsed around her and her husband; he was badly injured but survived. Also, two children in the Perry Mead family died. The oldest, a 12-year-old boy, was helping the youngest child, a 2-year-old, when they both fell into a crevasse that closed around them. The two middle children survived on the roof of the house.

Two people died in the collapse of the Penney's store downtown. Mary Louise Rustigan, a 40-year-old housewife, was fleeing from the store with her daughter along the side-walk when the corner of the building collapsed on top of her. The daughter was not caught in the debris. Also killed by falling concrete slabs outside the store was 18-year-old Lee Styer. Many accounts include the death of a woman crushed in her car by falling concrete, but she was rescued after the quake and survived.

The other four people who died in Anchorage included an air traffic controller crushed inside the collapsing control tower at the airport and a soldier at Fort Richardson who died in the hospital of a brain injury.

In addition to Turnagain, other landslides did major damage downtown. The 4th Avenue slide moved about 36 acres north some 17 feet, causing more than two blocks of businesses to collapse into a crater and damaging many others with ground subsidence, fractures and pressure ridges.

To the west along L Street, a piece of ground about 10 blocks long moved in one piece laterally about 10 feet. A six-story apartment building here slid with amazingly little damage.

In east downtown, the bluff behind the Native hospital slid away, destroying a fuel tank at the foot of the bluff, dropping the parking lot and hospital lawn about 25 feet, and doing some damage to the hospital.

The fifth big landslide occurred on Government Hill, where 400 feet of the bluff collapsed. The earth cracked open 1,180 feet wide under the school. The south wing dropped 30 feet and the east wing split lengthwise and collapsed. Soil from this slide traveled across the flats causing additional damage to Alaska Railroad facilities located there.

In the days following the quake, people mourned for the dead and gave thanks for their own survival. As displaced residents salvaged belongings from homes and businesses, city crews worked to restore water, power and sewer lines, reopen streets and demolish unsafe buildings. Health officials gave typhoid immunizations and relief agencies ran soup kitchens and distributed donated clothing that poured in from Outside. A federal commission was formed four days after the event to assist the state. Aftershocks continued for months, as the city received federal disaster funds and started rebuilding.

In Anchorage, a team of engineers identified unstable ground, including the L Street and 4th Avenue slide areas and recommended against rebuilding in these areas. Their report caused a great deal of controversy, particularly among landowners who did not want their property condemned at substantially lower post-quake values, and the task force's recommendations were generally disregarded. The only slide area stabilized was that on 4th Avenue. Using federal urban renewal funds, the clay was excavated and replaced with firmer soils and the area buttressed with a holding wall. While not stabilized, the Government Hill slide area where the school had been was made into a park.

Within six months of the quake, business-man Walter Hickel broke ground for his new Captain Cook Hotel, just east of the L Street landslide. He intentionally chose this location, he later said, to show confidence in downtown Anchorage and spur continued investments in the city. The L Street slide area was later rezoned for high-density development, despite geologists' assessment that the ground there has high potential for failure in another strong earthquake. Today 38 buildings, including several high rise structures, occupy this area; only the triangular, red Resolution Plaza was built to meet stricter building codes adopted in 1986.

In Turnagain, a few property owners accepted the city's offer of free lots on the east side of Anchorage in an area called Zodiak Manor. However, they were allowed to retain title to their Turnagain parcels. Discussions of stabilizing the area with urban renewal funds fizzled and died and within two years, the city council began considering applications for building permits in the bluff area. In 1975, the city restored the Turnagain properties to the tax rolls, and pressure to develop the slide area soon intensified.

The assembly appointed a committee to study the geotechnical hazards of the area and banned development pending the committee's findings. The committee's recommendation to buy the land and turn it into a park was rejected because of the cost, active opposition from the land owners and little community support. A small portion of the slide that sustained the worst damage was finally set aside as Earthquake Park.

By 1982, the property owners had formed improvement districts to redevelop the area

Movement from the earth split this large spruce in the Anchorage area. (Steve McCutcheon)

with water, sewer and roads, and the area was replatted to reestablish property lines. In the mid-1980s as the assembly moved to approve new construction, existing homeowners sued to stop it, concerned that building in the slide area would weaken their own homes and properties. This and other platting disputes were finally ended in 1990, when the improvement districts where allowed to proceed and sale of lots in the subdivision was permitted.

Today, large new homes are being built on these "view" lots in the Turnagain slide area. Developers and property owners in the slide area cite a 1989 study by the Shannon and Wilson engineering firm as evidence that the ground can be safely developed. The study concluded, among other things, that some consolidation of soils had occurred since the earthquake, and that the ground could support development. Still, questions about the area's stability remain, and some experts consider the area one of high seismic risk that should not have been redeveloped. In any event, new construction here must meet strict building codes designed to keep a house intact and standing should the ground underneath fail in the event of another great earthquake.

Little evidence of the 1964 earthquake remains visible in Anchorage now. The tumbled ground of Earthquake Park has eroded and become overgrown with trees and bushes, making landslide scars difficult to find. The 4th Avenue slide buttress area downtown has been rebuilt with a bright yellow mall, and the L Street slide area hosts apartment houses, high-rise office buildings and two of the city's finer restaurants with spectacular views across Cook Inlet. A sharp-eyed observer may look south down L Street from 4th Avenue in the early morning when traffic is light, however, and still see a bend at 9th Avenue, where the ground moved in 1964. ●

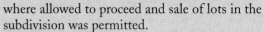

This aerial shows the slide area in the Turnagain district five years after the quake. (Steve McCutcheon)

Growing Up at Campbell Airstrip

By Scott Banks

Editor's note: *Scott manages public relations for the Alaska Railroad Corp.*

My earliest memory of Campbell Airstrip is of me careening down the road on the running boards of a 1956 red International pickup. It was the late 1960s and the military used the area, now called Far North Bicentennial Park, for maneuvers.

Our band of marauding scavengers was searching for anything left behind from the latest war games. Fox holes dotting the ridges held tossed-off C-rations, the occasional flashlight and blank ammunition that we used to make menacing-looking bandoliers.

The military completed construction of Campbell Airstrip in 1943 as one of four 5,000-foot satellite airfields for Fort Richardson and Elmendorf Field. The name Campbell comes from Point Campbell, which was first named in 1794 by Lt. Joseph Whidbey, probably for Sir Joseph Campbell, the governor of Jamaica in 1785 when Whidbey's superior, Capt. George Vancouver, was in the West Indies. Now the area is a park enjoyed by walkers, runners, orienteerers, skiers, dog mushers and skijorers.

Old tank trails intersect lakes, swamps, meadows, hills and dwindle out in the foothills of the Chugach Mountains. The airstrip, with

Zane, age 5, and Justin, age 7, enjoy a weekend outing with their dad, Scott Banks, near Campbell Airstrip. The bridge is a far cry from the rope that Scott used to cross the creek when he was a youngster. (Jody Karcz-Banks)

its overgrown taxiways, dominates the midwestern section. It's a wilderness amid Alaska's largest city.

When I was a youngster, the road into the area was a pickup-truck-and-a-half wide, dug into the gravel below the forest floor. A guard shack, by then vacant, pulled sentry duty at the entrance off Tudor Road.

On one adventure into the area, we stalked spruce hens. I armed myself with a weathered croquet ball. An unlucky flock crossed our path; I took hasty aim and let loose. A cloud of tail feathers exploded into the air, but feathers were my only reward. I was flush with brave daring, but inside I think I was secretly relieved at having missed.

During my first two years of high school, a friend and I used to run to Service High on the southern edge of the park. We'd trot down Baxter Road and cut through the site of an old chicken farm. A new subdivision with half-built houses enticed us for a closer look before we darted across Tudor Road. I now live in one of those houses.

About a mile down Campbell Airstrip Road, a 90-degree curve signaled our shortcut to Campbell Creek and a rope tied high up a birch tree limb. No bridges here. Daypacks strapped on, we'd swing across Tarzan-style.

With four miles of woods to our destination, distractions abounded. We missed entire school days. My mom invariably found out I missed school, but she rarely squawked. I think she knew I was doing harmless things.

On one journey near the creek, we spied a fairly intact parachute tangled in a cottonwood snag. We spent the rest of the day extracting the parachute. Some 20 years later, I still have ditty bags sewn from the parachute material.

I'm still exploring Campbell Airstrip. I run through the area, which abounds with wildlife. On one run, I ran to a trail that was posted off limits because of a nearby carcass of a bear-killed moose. I changed directions and trotted north along a ski trail toward Tudor Road. I came to a rise where I startled a falcon. It flew at me at waist level. I froze. At the last moment, it pulled up and settled onto a branch. It chirped, as I watched then inched my way slowly beneath it.

Thirty yards beyond it swooped at me again. I sensed something methodical and intent about its flight. This time I took refuge behind some spruce. I moved again, walking backwards and then turning and running. I'm not sure why, but I glanced back, and the falcon was coming at me one more time. At the last second, it veered off and flew into the forest. The encounter left me feeling wonder, fear and joy.

A mile beyond, a flock of spruce hens broke from cover

BELOW LEFT: *Canada dogwood (bunchberry) brightens the ground cover in Far North Bicentennial Park and adjacent Campbell Tract. The Bureau of Land Management manages the 730-acre Campbell Tract; the Municipality of Anchorage manages the 4,011-acre park. (Jon R. Nickles)*

BELOW: *Anchorage is likely the largest urban area to have a resident population of moose. Far North Bicentennial Park/ Campbell Tract provides habitat for several species of wildlife. (Jon R. Nickles)*

BELOW RIGHT: *Bog rosemary is a common heath family member found in Anchorage bogs. (Jon R. Nickles)*

and sent my heart pounding. Maybe it was their revenge for my sins long ago. This day of running did not relieve stress.

Now I have a family with two boys whom I'm introducing to the area. One of our first trips was to identify mushrooms. I learned children would rather kick the cap off a mushroom than identify it. This early parenting lesson showed me that nature teaches in her own way. Just as I learned, so too will my children through experience. We foray into the park with only vague intentions. Spontaneity provides all the study material we need.

Three miles up the road, at what we call Birch Tree, we follow the ski trail to find the south fork of Campbell Creek. Here it runs swiftly, hurrying to a gentler landscape below. The boys scurry to the creek to pick up rocks. My only worry is that one of them will chuck a rock into the back of the other's head. I spend my time poking around, watching

them, marveling that salmon spawn this high up the creek.

This area of birch, willow, alder and devil's club is prime for watching fall colors. To the east, Wolverine, O'Malley and Flat Top peaks provide a backdrop, black rock precipices soon to be blanketed by snow. My children don't notice, but give them time.

Several years ago hornets enjoyed a banner year. The boys and their friend took a walk to find nests, something I'd done as a kid. They weren't disappointed. It seemed every fifth tree held a nest, some bigger than a basketball. The boys buzzed about in constant motion, seeing who would locate the next one.

In early spring we took a walk to the creek, which was beginning to break up. The crusty snow lulled us into a false sense of security. We took tentative steps, then punched through up to our thighs. Bright reflecting snow and leafless trees allowed us to see farther through the forest than summer growth allows. While I preferred to sit and watch, the boys wanted to make dams and stir the water.

We followed tracks along the creek, probably coyote, checking out where the water peeked through the ice. My children ran from one spot to the next, quiet and absorbed, then broke out giggling. I realized this will always be their park. ●

The Hilltop Ski Area, in Hillside Park next to Far North Bicentennial Park on the southeast, provides downhill runs and cross-country trails for skiers. The two parks combined have more than 41 miles of trails; Campbell Tract has an additional 20-plus miles of trails. (Alaskana Photo-Art)

Big Bucks and
Bigger Government

A vortex of change swirled through Anchorage in the 1970s, much of it directly related to oil. This was the decade when oil took hold in Alaska, adding a dimension of wealth — and controversy — previously unimaginable.

Alaska's oil discoveries and pending pipeline construction had captured national and international attention, and Anchorage churned with upheaval. The city swelled with laborers and others anxiously awaiting work to start. But objections from conservation groups and Alaska Natives would stall the project, and the pipeline began to look like a pipe dream. Finally in 1975, construction got underway. Within two years, at a cost of nearly $9 billion, the 800-mile-long pipeline delivered its first load of North Slope crude to the terminal at Valdez. The state treasury ballooned with oil revenues, and Anchorage received a hefty share.

This chapter looks at how pipeline construction and the early rush of oil played in Anchorage, along with a few of the other less spectacular, but still notable, events of the decade.

The North Slope oil lease sale started the state swimming in money. The invested proceeds were generating

LEFT: *Winter doesn't stop Anchorage residents from enjoying their hot tubs. (Alissa Crandall)*

FACING PAGE: *The municipality's extensive trail system, 13 major multiple-use trails running more than 100 miles, encourages cross-country skiers to stretch their muscles. These skiers enjoy the coastal trail. The trail system got its start in the early 1970s when Lanie Fleischer, a trails advocate who had recently moved here from Washington DC, and Judge John Reese began to push for bike trails to get around the city without driving a car. The first trail, from Westchester Lagoon to Goose Lake along Chester Creek, was renamed the Lanie Fleischer Chester Creek Trail in 1994. (Alissa Crandall)*

Downtown Anchorage

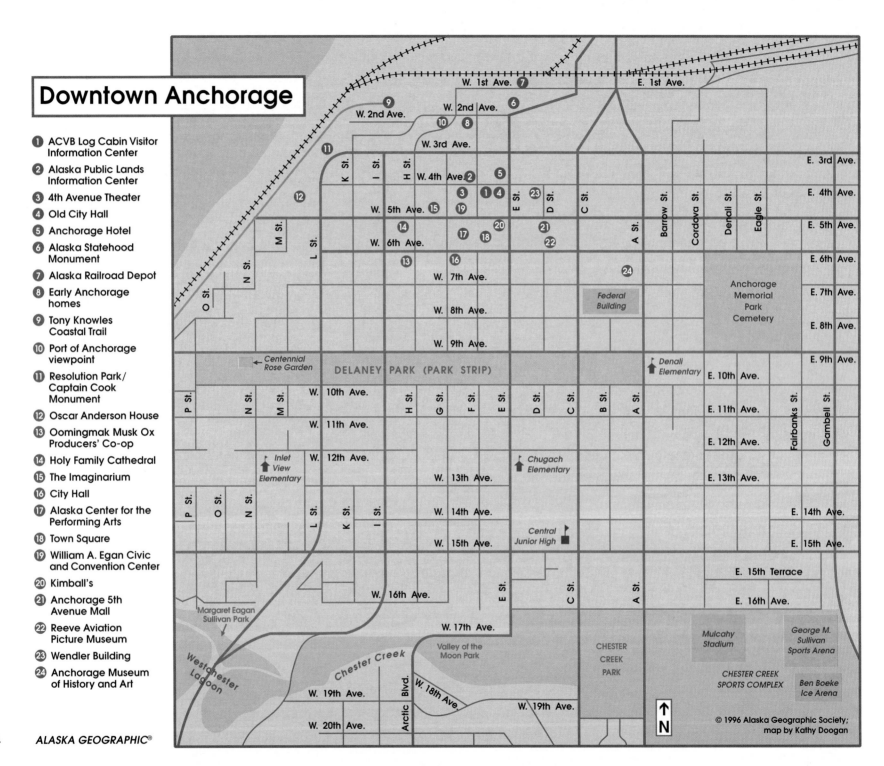

1. ACVB Log Cabin Visitor Information Center
2. Alaska Public Lands Information Center
3. 4th Avenue Theater
4. Old City Hall
5. Anchorage Hotel
6. Alaska Statehood Monument
7. Alaska Railroad Depot
8. Early Anchorage homes
9. Tony Knowles Coastal Trail
10. Port of Anchorage viewpoint
11. Resolution Park/ Captain Cook Monument
12. Oscar Anderson House
13. Oomingmak Musk Ox Producers' Co-op
14. Holy Family Cathedral
15. The Imaginarium
16. City Hall
17. Alaska Center for the Performing Arts
18. Town Square
19. William A. Egan Civic and Convention Center
20. Kimball's
21. Anchorage 5th Avenue Mall
22. Reeve Aviation Picture Museum
23. Wendler Building
24. Anchorage Museum of History and Art

© 1996 Alaska Geographic Society; map by Kathy Doogan

Strip malls had reached the Jewel Lake area of southwest Anchorage by the mid-1970s. (Pete K. Martin)

$187,500 a day by December 1969, and that didn't include the state's anticipated share of millions of dollars from oil still in the ground. As 1970 dawned, construction seemed imminent. Many people were practically giddy with the thought of big bucks to be made in the opportunities ahead.

Sections of 48-inch-diameter pipe started arriving on ships from Japan, and loads of pipe traveled by railcar through Anchorage to Fairbanks. A 27-foot section of pipe even adorned the City Hall lawn in downtown Anchorage, although the actual pipeline route wouldn't come within 150 miles of town.

Not everyone was happy about the thought of Alaska awash in oil. Alaska Natives had picketed outside the Sydney Laurence Auditorium downtown during the state's oil lease sale with signs that read, "$2,000,000,000 Native Land Robbery." The Natives had been fighting with the federal government for land since the early 1960s and now extended their aboriginal claims to the pipeline corridor. Some of them also worried that development would affect the caribou and fish they hunted. A federal judge ruled that their claims had to be settled before pipeline construction could proceed.

At the same time, conservation groups led by the Sierra Club and Wilderness Society filed suit to stop the project, because of its potential environmental harm. They said the project failed to meet provisions of the newly enacted National Environmental Policy Act, which required environmental impact statements for any projects affecting federal lands.

The matter bogged down in court. "Day by day the picture seems to get darker," state Rep. Tom Fink, of Anchorage, told fellow legislators in June 1970.

"Is it time for Alaskans to consider the possibility the proposed Prudhoe Bay-to-Valdez pipeline may never be built?" asked the *Anchorage Daily News.*

Anchorage meantime thronged with transient laborers looking for jobs on what was to be the biggest private construction project in the nation's history, estimated in the beginning to cost $900 million and employ 13,000 workers. Oil company executives and managers were relocating to Anchorage to run new corporate offices. "Spurred by the oil boom, new arrivals have reversed the old trend which saw an exodus of seasonal workers to the south as winter approached," noted an *Alaska Magazine* article drawn from 1970 news reports.

With several hundred new students arriving each month, elementary schools started double shifts to accommodate all the children. The Federal Housing Authority reported that 3,000 new living quarters in Anchorage would be needed just to stay even with the population boom. Trailer parks proliferated.

Jobs did not. Unemployment in Anchorage skyrocketed.

"Don't come…without a definite job offer," warned the state labor department.

Realizing that Native land claims had to be settled, the oil companies joined the Alaska Federation of Natives to lobby Congress. Lawmakers responded in 1971 and passed the Alaska Native Land Claims Settlement Act. This revolutionary settlement granted Alaska's Natives nearly 43 million acres of land and $962.5 million, and established 12 regional corporations and 220 village corporations to manage the land and money. On Dec. 16, 1971, hundreds of Native leaders met at Alaska Methodist University and voted to accept the terms.

Now oil development hinged on the environmental questions and the nation's looming energy crisis. In Anchorage, hundreds of Alaskans turned out to testify for and against the pipeline during five days of hearings before federal officials. "A parade of state legislators, mayors, councilmen and Chamber of Commerce members asked for early issuance of a construction permit," reported *Alaska Magazine*. Supporters predicted dire economic conse-quences for the state and the nation if the project was abandoned; detractors called the pipeline "a monstrous tube" and Alaska's undoing. "The pipeline is totally bad news," said David Brower, president of Friends of the Earth. "The most valuable thing here is the extraordinary stand of the last great wilderness."

Finally in November 1973, President Richard Nixon signed into law a bill authorizing pipeline construction.

If Anchorage's growth had sputtered from the delays, it now took off. By fall 1974, the city's population boomed to 79,000, with about 162,500 people living between Chugiak and Girdwood. More job seekers flooded town. Although much of the hiring was done out of Fairbanks, Anchorage was the point of arrival for most. Anchorage the corporate oil headquarters now became labor union headquarters. At one point, the city had about 30 unions.

The most powerful and wealthiest of the unions was Teamsters Union Local 959, with about 23,000 members. During this time, under leadership of former truck driver Jesse Carr, the Teamsters built a mall on Debarr Road for union offices and medical facilities. Teamsters Pension Fund money also financed in part a new building for Anchorage Community Hospital, today Columbia Alaska Regional Hospital. The union also built a huge recreation center on Tudor Road for its members, which today is the Alaska Club. The Teamster's power and politics were investigated by *Anchorage Daily News* reporter Howard Weaver; his series of articles won the paper a Pulitzer Prize in 1976.

Dani Lavictoire, Austin Nolfi and Emma Lohr plant flowers on a protective berm at a busy corner of the Business Park Wetland in midtown. The students from Denali Elementary School are part of Cami Dalton's class that took on the area as a year-long project. The wetland, purchased with public and private money, was selected as valuable habitat because of its density of nesting Canada geese, gulls and other bird species. (L.J. Campbell, staff)

RIGHT: *Downhill skiers can choose from Hilltop Ski Area or Arctic Valley on the eastern edge of town, or drive south on the Seward Highway to Girdwood and the year-round resort of Alyeska. (Danny Daniels)*

BELOW RIGHT: *Fog blankets upper Cook Inlet and much of Anchorage, accentuating Mount Susitna, 4,396 feet, usually called Sleeping Lady, across the inlet. (Alaskana Photo-Art)*

As pipeline construction hit full force, its spin-off impact on "booming Fairbanks and Anchorage is so great that new building projects make aerial photos obsolete after 24 hours," according to a news report at the time.

Major construction projects of this decade included a $13 million expansion of Providence Hospital, which had moved after the quake to land adjoining the college campus; a $6 million addition to the Anchorage Westward Hotel increasing its capacity by 600 rooms; a new 14-story Royal Inn, a 250-room Holiday Inn and a 375-room Sheraton; a new office building for Union Oil; expansion of the Atlantic Richfield building; and a 10-story headquarters for Cook Inlet Region Inc., one of the new Native regional corporations. The University Center mall went in, and McDonald's and the Post Office Mall were built on the buttress area downtown, with the yellow Sunshine Mall a few years later. J.C. Penney was expanded and Nordstrom department store opened in the renovated Northern Commercial Co. building. In 1976, construction began on a $71 million federal building complex between A and C streets downtown. News reports even told that Texas oil millionaire H.L. Hunt was looking to Anchorage to possibly build a "giant downtown complex of 20-story office buildings, hotel and retail stores" in addition to having purchased 66 lots in the Anchorage bowl.

A survey conducted by a political consulting firm during this period, however, revealed city residents to be in an "anti-development mood. Forty percent of those

interviewed said Anchorage was developed enough; only 13 percent felt more was needed.

Anchorage was growing in other ways, too. A satellite put into orbit for Alaska enabled the city to get live television for the first time in January 1971, with the Super Bowl and the Apollo moon flight among the first programs beamed down.

Anchorage also got its second four-year college offering graduate and post-graduate degrees when University of Alaska opened a branch on land leased from Alaska Methodist University. The two universities agreed not to duplicate each other's courses, but AMU was unable to compete with the lower tuitions charged by the state-subsidized university and closed in 1976. It reopened the next year as Alaska Pacific University under the leadership of Dr. Glenn Olds, former president of Kent State University in Ohio.

The airport was expanded, with direct jet service initiated between Anchorage and Houston, home offices to many of the oil companies. A fall bow and arrow season was opened for moose, to keep the runways clear.

Anchorage's streets reached farther into the bowl. The Spenard Throughway, which ran between Northern Lights Boulevard and 15th Avenue, was extended to International Airport Road and renamed the Minnesota Bypass. Seward Highway and C Street were expanded, Tudor Road was widened to four lanes — a bumpy, muddy project that

ABOVE LEFT: *With several months of winter and a close relationship with the North Pole, Anchorageites make the most of their decorative skills during the holiday season. (Harry M. Walker)*

LEFT: *Because of its central location atop the North Pacific rim, Anchorage has become an important transshipment point for international delivery services. Federal Express maintains a major hub at Anchorage International Airport. (Steve McCutcheon)*

The Air Force, Army and several other military units play a big role in Anchorage's economy and society. Each summer Elmendorf Air Force Base holds an open house where the public is invited for a closer look at some of the Air Force's planes. These visitors are inspecting a C-5A Galaxy, the largest plane in the fleet. (Department of the Air Force)

resurrected the "I drove Tudor Road" bumper stickers — and Muldoon was four-laned. Yet a stop sign still stood at the corner of Lake Otis and Northern Lights. Only a few homes dotted the Hillside, and little was on O'Malley except the zoo. Several restaurants catered to downtown diners. Away from downtown, two popular places to eat at the time were the Alaskaland ice cream parlor and an A-frame owned by Tony Knowles called Grizzly Burger, catty corner from each other at the intersection of Northern Lights and C streets.

Several other events worth noting occurred during the '70s. Voters finally approved the capital move in 1974 by a 3-to-2 margin, after language was included prohibiting the new capital from being closer than 30 miles to either Fairbanks or Anchorage. In 1976, the community of Willow, located 35 air miles north of Anchorage, was chosen as the new capital site with the move to be completed by 1980. The euphoria of victory for Anchorage capital-move supporters and land speculators was short-lived, however. Six years later, voters decided to leave the capital in Juneau when faced with the astronomical cost of the proposed move.

Meanwhile, a battle of another sort was erupting in Anchorage. On Nov. 10, 1970, more than 300 people crowded into the Sydney Laurence Auditorium to protest city plans to annex a vast area, including Muldoon, Fort Richardson and Elmendorf Air Force Base. The city would increase from 16.5 square miles to almost 600, nearly double its population and get more than half a million dollars a year additional in state funds.

The annexation effort, which later succeeded with the military bases, was part of a bigger local issue — combining the city and borough into a single, unified government. It was a matter that had been debated, at times hotly, since the borough's formation in 1964 under state law. Many people outside the city, who had fought higher taxes and regulations, now resisted borough governance. Many of the city leaders also viewed the borough with suspicion as a competing government agency. The 11-member borough assembly was split between representatives from the city's assembly and the borough, with the majority coming from the largest population base. Borough meetings were lively affairs in rooms packed with vocal audiences, remembers second borough Mayor Jack Roderick, who served from 1972 until 1975.

The idea of combining city and borough governments took on urgency as the city-borough squabbles threatened to freeze both governments completely. A citizens'

committee formed to study the issue and Operation Breakthrough, composed of 600 people, recommended action. Two votes on unification in 1970 and 1971 failed by a 2-1 margin, rejected overwhelmingly by people outside the city limits. But the growth of the borough from newcomers with different attitudes, plus growing disgust with the current state of affairs, finally brought about a successful unification vote in 1975.

As the new unified government began sorting out its path under Mayor George Sullivan, Anchorage started receiving money from the state like never before. Oil started flowing through the pipeline in 1977, and its revenues would become the major source of funding for all sorts of projects. Among other things, some of Anchorage's first oil money went into arts and by 1978, 48 percent of the city's residents were participating in some kind of fine arts activity, according to the National Research Center of Arts. The municipal assembly enacted a 1-percent-for-art program, requiring all public structures costing more than $250,000 to earmark 1 percent of construction costs for art purchases. This gave Alaska artists a lucrative new market and brought many museum-quality art pieces into public view. The program continues today. ■

Boom and Bust

Extremes rocked Anchorage in the 1980s. The decade opened in wealth, with oil revenues fueling state spending like never before. Anchorage boomed with unprecedented affluence, and quality of life took on new meaning as Project '80s, a massive construction project of public buildings and recreational facilities, got underway. Then oil prices crashed, plunging Anchorage into its worst-ever recession. People lost their jobs and their homes, and caravans of families driving U-Hauls snaked along the highway out. By decade's end, the city had started recovering. Oil again played a part, this time bringing work cleaning up the *Exxon Valdez* oil spill in Prince William Sound.

Former Anchorage Mayor George Sullivan, who served from 1967 through 1982, thought that the state's oil income should buy something long-lasting and useful. His vision resulted in Project '80s, an ambitious public building project for Anchorage that molded the city's modern appearance, function and attitude.

To recap briefly, Sullivan remembers the pre-pipeline days of the early 1970s as rough times in Anchorage. Local business owners had increased their inventories to supply pipeline construction, in some cases borrowing heavily, and the delays created financial problems and some bankruptcies. The town was crowded with unemployed, destitute

LEFT: *Beginning in the early 1980s, when this photo was taken, the state undertook a multiyear program to upgrade the Seward Highway, which runs from Anchorage to Seward on Resurrection Bay. The improvements continue in the mid-1990s, but even with the upgrades, heavy summer weekend use can halt traffic. (Alissa Crandall)*

FACING PAGE: *Any number of sightseeing companies stand ready to accommodate visitors in downtown Anchorage. (Chlaus Lotscher)*

ABOVE: *"Racing in the Footsteps of a Legend," a bronze sculpture of a running sled dog, stops pedestrians along 4th Avenue. (Harry M. Walker)*

ABOVE RIGHT: *The pride of downtown shoppers is the Fifth Avenue Mall, four floors of shops topped by a food court. The mall opens into J.C. Penney at its west end, and is connected to Nordstrom and to a parking garage by enclosed overstreet walkways. (Harry M. Walker)*

newcomers expecting to find work. The city scraped to provide services from its limited budget, funded mostly by property taxes; voters had repeatedly rejected sales taxes. Sullivan thought the state should share its pending oil wealth with local governments, and he helped instigate two programs still active today — state revenue sharing and municipal assistance. When construction finally started, things got really crazy. About this time, the city and borough unification passed, and Sullivan was re-elected as mayor of the new municipality.

In the months that followed as the two governments melded, Sullivan started envisioning a new project. Oil was about to start flowing through the pipeline, generating billions of dollars of new revenue. Some of it would be stashed in the newly created Alaska Permanent Fund, designed as a long-term savings account to pay annual dividends on earnings to Alaskans. But Sullivan wanted a share of the oil money for Anchorage to use for something long-lasting that people could point to and say, "This is what our oil money bought." He and his staff started brainstorming. They met in the evenings, on weekends. They talked to people in the community. They looked at what Anchorage had and what it needed.

They came up with a long list of capital improvements, everything from a convention center, sports arena, performing arts center and new library to recreation centers, a coastal trail from Eagle River to Girdwood, and a "railroad town" tourist attraction with historic log cabins at Ship Creek. Part of the idea behind Project '80s was to keep downtown alive, as well as to make the city attractive to

BELOW LEFT: *In 1988 a 1,200-vehicle parking garage and underground corridors connecting the garage and domestic terminal were completed at Anchorage International Airport. Plans call for additional upgrades to the domestic terminal beginning in 1996 with vacation of C Concourse and demolition of the wing in 1997. On the drawing board but at least five years away is a planned major expansion of the domestic terminal. (Harry M. Walker)*

BELOW: *Motorists entering Anchorage on the Glenn Highway are greeted by this welcome. (Harry M. Walker)*

FACING PAGE: *The premier resort in the Anchorage bowl is Alyeska at Girdwood, showcased by The Westin Alyeska Prince Hotel, which sports full facilities including several restaurants. One of its dining venues, which offers a spectacular view of the Girdwood Valley and Turnagain Arm, is reached by an enclosed tram up Mount Alyeska. (Harry M. Walker)*

RIGHT: *Population booms have spawned large trailer parks, designed to meet Anchorage's periodic housing shortages. (Ernest Manewal)*

visitors and to improve the quality of life for residents in the areas of culture, recreation and transportation.

They went to the state legislature for money. It was a hard sell at first, remembers Sullivan, but in 1980, the legislature granted the city $157 million. The next year with the majority of townspeople supporting Project '80s, Anchorage got additional grants of $235 million.

Limited to two terms by the Municipal charter, Sullivan was succeeded in office by young Vietnam veteran and businessman Tony Knowles. As mayor, Knowles added to the capital projects list in the areas of recreation, public safety, economic development, clean water, transportation and neighborhood enhancements. From 1982 through 1987 under Knowles, the city's capital construction budget topped $1 billion. During his administration, most of the original Project '80s items were completed, but not without some controversy as to budget, location or design. Still, many of Anchorage's most distinctive landmark buildings rose during this time.

The original Project '80s buildings included: the William A. Egan Civic and Convention Center, the biggest of its kind in the state; the Alaska Center for the Performing Arts, which replaced and incorporated the exterior wall of the old Sydney Laurence Auditorium; Town Square and other pedestrian amenities downtown; major expansion of the Anchorage Museum of History and Art; a new Loussac Library, which originally included a circular parking garage with covered entrances into the main library and the Alaska Collection (the garage was later axed for cost containment and replaced with exterior stairs hazardous in winter); the George M. Sullivan Sports Arena, the first major capital projects building named after someone; a large city transit facility and a new animal control building on Tudor Road; Dempsey Anderson ice arena and Spenard Recreation Center in west Anchorage; an Olympic-sized swimming pool at Bartlett High School; a golf course, equestrian center, ski area and trail system on the Hillside, expansion of Kincaid Park with land, trails, ski jumps and chalet; Fire Lake ice arena in Eagle River; expansion of the Senior Center in Chugiak; and the Tony Knowles Coastal Trail.

The capital projects were perhaps the most visible sign of Anchorage's astronomical growth and affluence during the first half of the 1980s. Alaska, overall, was undergoing a tremendous boom as the state pumped billions of dollars from oil revenues into the economy. By 1982, the state had collected $12 billion in oil taxes and royalties and was spending about $8,500 per person, almost three times as much as the federal government was spending per American.

By 1981, Anchorage was growing by 1,000 people a month, part of a population increase of 40 percent during the early 1980s. Employment in Anchorage jumped 43 percent during this time. By 1980, retail and wholesale trade and services were employing almost as many people as government, which traditionally had been the city's largest

employer. Anchorage residents had personal incomes almost twice as high as the national average. In 1980, the median income for an Anchorage household was $37,511; by 1985, it was $48,163. Anchorageites and other Alaskans enjoyed their personal pay-off from oil development when the first Alaska Permanent Fund dividend checks, at $1,000 each, were issued in fall 1982.

Anchorage also experienced a housing boom of unrealized impact. During the first five years of the decade, 25,000 new units were built, an increase in housing stock of 40 percent. Condominiums sprang up all over town, and residential sprawl extended into south Anchorage and onto the Hillside.

A comprehensive plan for Anchorage's development was adopted in about 1982, based in part on recommendations regarding seismic hazards developed after the 1964 earthquake. However, the subject was still quite sensitive. In the final draft, all references to not developing the slide areas were removed as were all mentions of the word "earthquake."

As one of the fastest growing cities in the nation in the early 1980s, Anchorage was a desirable place to live. Recreation, long a priority with residents, bloomed under generous city funding, about 15 percent of the tax-supported budget directed to this area. The city's greenbelts and trails, which had started being developed in the 1970s, expanded with 100 miles of paved trails connecting neighborhoods, schools and dozens of parks. In 1983, the city hosted the Nordic World Cup and National Ski Championship, and the University of Alaska started hosting the Great Alaska Shootout, an invitational basketball tournament for top-ranked college teams. Delaney Park downtown gained new tennis courts, horseshoe pits,

In the 1980s, Anchorage bid to host a winter Olympics in the 1990s. It lost the bid, but did lure a number of international winter competitions to the city, such as the Olympic Biathlon trials. (Alaskana Photo-Art)

volleyball courts, a rebuilt hockey rink and lighted figure-skating rink.

It was also a city of arts, with about 70 performing groups and 30 art galleries by 1983. People here loved movies, as well, as evidenced by the presence of 12 theaters; in 1981, Anchorage movie goers spent more than $5 million.

In addition to the capital projects and new homes, the construction boom also included several large privately financed ventures, such as ARCO Alaska's high-rise office tower downtown, British Petroleum's large new office complex on east Northern Lights, the Frontier Building in midtown, the Alaska Federal Credit Union, the Alaska Mutual Building, and the Hunt (Enserch) Building, Resolution Tower and a mall downtown.

But by the time the mall opened, in August 1987, the economy was in shambles

Oil prices plunged in spring 1986, triggering a recession of previously unequaled proportions for Anchorage. As early as 1982, oil prices had drifted downward, and by mid-1985, state spending had dropped. The resulting economic slowdown was felt particularly in construction. But the price crash was to the economy what the '64 earthquake had been to the ground. It toppled everything.

Between 1987 and 1989, Alaska lost 20,000 jobs. Real estate values collapsed, dropping more than 50 percent in some cases. People found themselves with no incomes and overpriced homes they couldn't pay for or sell for what they owed. Thousands of homeowners defaulted

LEFT AND FACING PAGE: *By its 75th anniversary in 1990, Anchorage had become a mature city, with high rises, parks and an expansive setting on the lowlands beneath the Chugach Mountains.*

At left, a vista of water and mountains dominates this scene looking west over downtown. The park strip stretches toward Knik Arm, with snow-topped Mount Susitna at right and the snow-covered Alaska-Aleutian Range in the distance. Denali Elementary School is at the lower end of the park strip, the Federal Building is the light-colored building with its windows appearing as horizontal stripes, the museum is to the Federal Building's right and the Fifth Avenue Mall is the light brown building at center connected by a skywalk to a parking garage to its right.

On the facing page, looking east over downtown, the brown Captain Cook Hotel stands at left center, the ARCO and Enserch towers at center and the park strip at right. (Both by Alissa Crandall)

on mortgages; lenders foreclosed on nearly 1,200 homes and condominiums between 1988 and 1989 alone. But the previous construction boom had left Anchorage's financial institutions overextended, and eight banks closed during the crash.

Anchorage reeled as thousands of people left the area and headed out of state. "Every time you went up town, you heard of somebody else getting hurt," said Sullivan.

By late 1988, the crisis was easing somewhat. People who still had jobs were, in many cases, taking advantage of the real estate crash to buy bigger homes, or buy for the first time, at bargain prices. In general, wages in the surviving job market had increased and median household incomes in

Anchorage were back up almost to 1985 levels. Although the cost of living was 15 percent higher in Anchorage than the national average, it was down considerably from years earlier, largely due to lower housing costs. And taxes were about the lowest in the nation. In interviews conducted that year by the Institute for Social and Economic Research at the University of Alaska, many Anchorage residents said that their situation had improved from the previous year, but they thought others were faring more poorly.

Then came the *Exxon Valdez* oil spill in Prince William Sound, the nation's largest tanker spill. It occurred on March 27, 1989, 25 years to the day after the earthquake. Anchorage escaped the oil spill's devastation suffered by many of Alaska's southern coastal communities. It benefited, however, from the resulting cleanup, which was a major force in economic recovery throughout the railbelt. About 6 percent of Anchorage's households reported that they had at least one member who worked directly in the oil spill clean up sometime in 1989. ■

Anchorage's Public Gardens

By Jill Shepherd

Editor's note: *Jill is senior editor for* Alaska Magazine.

Tourists probably expend as much camera film on the outstanding public floral displays around Anchorage as they do on elusive Mount McKinley, and with good reason. From dahlias as big as dinner plates seen in Town Square to rare Himalayan blue poppies found at the Alaska Botanical Garden, the flowers are remarkable for their intense colors and large size. What's also noteworthy is that public landscaping and flower beds are relative newcomers to this frontier city.

In just 81 years, Anchorage has grown from a railroad tent city built on Ship Creek clay to the sprawling metropolis it is today. Along the way this northern community has developed an appetite for flowers.

Last year Anchorage Parks and Recreation maintained 50 landscaped parks and 571 flower beds at 66 sites throughout the city, including 60 lineal-lane miles of landscaped roadways. No other city in the state has the financial means

nor the hundreds of volunteer gardeners to support a beautification program on such a grand scale.

In 1995 the municipal greenhouses grew 65,000 annuals for their display gardens. Already in bloom when transplanted outdoors in early June, the flowers transform the city almost overnight. The plantings have been dubbed "instant gardens" and satisfy residents' need for a quick color fix after a white winter.

Dubbed by some the "Hanging Flower Basket Capital of the World," Anchorage's city gardeners put out 320 baskets of lobelia and marigolds in 1995. This string hangs from recently installed, old-style streetlights, both designed to give downtown's 4th Avenue the look of Anchorage in an earlier era. (Harry M. Walker)

Some of the more prominent flower gardens are listed below.

Log Cabin Visitor Information Center
F Street and 4th Avenue

Wild onions growing on the sod roof of this picturesque cabin in the downtown district are reminiscent of Anchorage's "vegetable heritage," when homesteaders would plant the vegetable garden on the roof, out of reach of marauding moose. Look for other vegetables, like cabbage and kale, which are found in most of the city's gardens.

The informal flower beds surrounding the cabin display an assortment of flowers that includes tuberous begonia, alyssum, dahlia, delphinium, fuchsia, geranium, nicotiana, zinnia, and ornamental cabbage and kale.

This busy corner is a good spot to start photographing flowers, including the city's hanging flower baskets that are placed along 2nd, 3rd and 4th avenues. Last year the city

After a marathon battle to convince city officials that voters really meant what they said, Anchorage finally got its Town Square, a gracefully landscaped, flower-filled square between 5th and 6th avenues. (Danny Daniels)

planted 320 baskets with blue lobelia and gold marigolds, the colors of the city of Anchorage and state of Alaska. The city often is referred to as the "Hanging Flower Basket Capital of the World." Homeowners and commercial establishments hang an estimated 60,000 baskets every year.

Town Square
5th and 6th avenues bordered by E Street

Shadowed by the Alaska Center for the Performing Arts on the west end of the block, Town Square is a riot of color, with 13 flower beds planted with 7,600 annuals. Noteworthy in the 1995 display were 15 varieties of marigolds, eight kinds of tuberous begonias, three different delphinium and five impatiens. Two cabbages were featured: the ornamental "Rose Bouquet" and the edible "Savoy King."

Anchorage Museum of History and Art
121 W. 7th Avenue

The permanent history and art collections within the museum are the city's top visitor attraction, but during the summer the seven flower beds surrounding the building attract equal attention. Filled with 3,000 plants, the beds feature 91 varieties in colors so vibrant they seem to pulsate. The rainbow array includes dahlias with exotic names like "Arabian Night," Black Narcissus" and "Awaioke," which share the spotlight with geraniums, impatiens, 14 kinds of pansies, 15 different snapdragons, two varieties of ornamental cabbage, six varieties of ornamental kale, and one edible cabbage named "Ruby Perfection."

L Street Hillside Picture
L Street (runs one-way south) at 15th Avenue

Since 1965, 30 different designs have appeared on the hillside above the road. Plants used to create last year's salmon theme included alyssum, begonia, lobelia and pansy.

Each summer a riot of color surrounds the Anchorage Museum of History and Art. Here, lunchtime finds children gathered along the A Street side of the museum, which is flanked by vibrant beds of snapdragons, geraniums, petunias and other flowers. (Harry M. Walker)

Mann Leiser Memorial Greenhouses
At the entrance to Russian Jack Springs Park
5200 DeBarr Road
Open 8 a.m. to 3 p.m. daily, except holidays

Gardeners can check out new outdoor flower varieties in the All-American Selection Display Garden, near the entrance to the greenhouse. One of the 1995 selections included a new class of petunia named "Purple Wave," the first petunia with a ground-cover habit. The display changes every year.

In addition to growing plants for use out-doors in the summer, the municipal greenhouses contain a small aviary and a permanent, tropical plant collection. Thousands of schoolchildren tour the solarium, and an average of 100 to 200 visitors make their way through the jungle habitat every month. Particularly in the winter, people like the trees, flowers and humid atmosphere. The solarium also is a popular place for weddings; about a hundred ceremonies take place every year to the gentle sounds of water bubbling in the pond and birds chirping in the aviary.

A visit to the solarium on Oct. 22 last fall revealed a number of plants in bloom, including bird of paradise, yellow shrimp plant, a Baja red fairy duster, double hibiscus, pink bougainvillea, lipstick plant and a *Brugmansia candida*, a tree with huge 5-by-8-inch trumpet-shaped blooms.

Gardens and flower plots decorate several-block-long Delaney Park, known to most Anchorage residents as the park strip. The city's Rose Garden has been planted near the west end of the strip. The park itself is named for James J. Delaney, three-term mayor of Anchorage from 1929 to 1931. (Harry M. Walker)

The Centennial Rose Garden
West end of Delaney Park
Between 9th and 10th avenues

Few people realize that the 200 rose bushes in this lovely summer garden spend winters in an unheated concrete bunker at an abandoned Nike missile site in Kincaid Park. Everything but the hardy rose hedge is portable, planted in three-gallon nursery pots. When stored for the winter in the bunker, the pots are laid horizontally on 2-inch-thick Styrofoam and covered with a thick layer of wood chips.

In mid-April the pots are moved outside and covered with clear plastic for six weeks. Ready for display by Memorial Day, the roses are at their peak by mid-July.

The rose garden was established in 1967 to commemorate Alaska's purchase from Russia in 1867.

Alaska Botanical Garden
Tudor Road at Campbell Airstrip Road
Summer hours: 9 a.m. to 9 p.m.

Probably the only botanical garden in the world with a dog mushing trail running through it, the Alaska Botanical Garden is located in the foothills of the Chugach Range. More than 300 plant acquisitions are displayed in a perennial garden and a demonstration garden, the only two gardens established since the non-profit venture opened in 1993. The remainder of the 110-acre site is a varied, natural terrain, with birch the dominant tree species.

One of the rare and unusual plants found in the perennial garden is the Himalayan blue poppy, which was in full bloom Aug. 6.

"There are very few true-blue flowers in the world," says Debbie Hinchey, past president of the Alaska Botanical Garden. "People see it and want to grow it in their gardens." The gardens also contain three varieties of lewisia, which, according to Hinchey, "is one of the 10 favorite plants on gardeners' wish lists around the world."

Visitors can take a self-guided tour along the broad footpaths that link the gardens together. Points of interest include the glacial erratics, rocks that have been carried long distances to the site by glaciers.

Two gardens have already been developed within the overall Alaska Botanical Garden, founded in 1993. Next on the agenda for the garden's planners is an herb garden. (Jill Shepherd)

Planting in 1996 will include an herb garden and an edible garden based on gardens planted by the early Russians on Kodiak Island in 1794. Like the Chinese, who cultivated parklike gardens for their emperors some 4,000 years ago, Alaskans love their gardens. ●

A Mature Metropolis

Anchorage today could hardly be imagined by the early pioneer homesteaders, or the railroad engineers who laid out the town, or the Dena'ina (Tanaina) Indians who hunted and fished here before them. Even its early boosters who championed the military and government and oil could not have imagined the city's most recent incarnation.

Anchorage has become in the 1990s a city of store clerks and shoppers, of low-paid part-time jobs and more things to buy than money to spend. WalMarts and K-Marts, warehouse groceries and giant specialty outlets give Anchorage a new look, the most obvious change characterizing this modern city not yet a century old.

Fly into the city for the first time, and it's easy to see how close Anchorage is to the edge. After hours over glaciers and wilderness coastline, the plane starts descending. Passengers peer out the windows, anxiously looking for a place to land but seeing only mountainous ice fields. The last steep ridge of white finally drops away, and a grid of roads and buildings appears across a wedge of flatlands. As the plane swings out over Cook Inlet to approach the airport, the high-rise buildings of downtown glint in the sun. Some 257,000 people — nearly half the state's population — live here. It is Alaska's largest city. Yet dwarfed by the surrounding wilderness and isolated by distance, Anchorage seems small and tenuous.

It's a fleeting impression. The city is geographically large, stretching from Eklutna on the north to Girdwood on the south. It encompasses nearly 2,000 square miles, only about 200 of which are inhabited. The majority of Anchorage is

LEFT: *Alaskans consume more ice cream per capita than do the residents of any other state. (Alaskana Photo-Art)*

FACING PAGE: *Strollers enjoy the afternoon sun along the shore of Knik Arm below the coastal trail. (Danny Daniels)*

parklands and forests. It has a greenbelt and trail system unsurpassed by any city in the nation. The trails fill with people on foot, bikes and roller blades, and horseback in summer, on skis and behind dogs sleds in winter.

They share the trails with resident moose, who always get the right-of-way. It's not unusual to see moose browsing in the fields out by the airport, near the Federal Express package handling facility and hangars, or bedded down on the university lawn, or meandering through a neighborhood. Winter brings them to dine on tasty ornamental plantings such as mountain ash trees and lilacs bushes. When the snow is exceptionally deep, moose have been known to step right up on rooftops and browse birch overhangs. People still meet up with bears and wolves on the city's fringe. Occasionally a young bruin will follow the green belt into the city; several years ago, a bear came out of the Chester Creek greenbelt onto E Street where it was shot dead in a parking lot a few blocks from downtown by Fish and Game staff.

Meanwhile, Anchorage's peopled parcels are being increasingly developed.

The city in the early 1990s was undergoing a construction boom not seen for nearly a decade. This included numerous publicly funded projects, such as six new schools, a state court high-rise downtown, a new Native hospital and medical center, and a new hospital on Elmendorf. But a more fundamental change occurred when the national retailers descended.

They blanketed Anchorage with discount department stores, wholesale warehouses and specialty outlets: K-Marts, WalMarts, Sam's Club, Costcos, Paces, Eagle Hardware, Borders Books and Music, Fred Meyers, Office Max, Sports Authority for starters. The onslaught has brought hundreds of new jobs, but they're mostly part-time and low-wage, particularly when compared to Anchorage's traditional employment in government, military and more recently oil. Federal budget cuts have tightened government hiring and resulted in a small exodus of military, although Anchorage so far has been spared base closures. Convoys of camouflage trucks still travel the Glenn Highway, hauling Army soldiers to training exercises. Fighter jet formations routinely pattern the skies above town; air shows at Elmendorf draws large crowds. The military's presence is perhaps less evident as the city has grown, but now, for the first time, more military families live in the city than on base. The oil companies have also cut back in the last several years. ARCO, formerly Atlantic Richfield, and British Petroleum trimmed their highly paid workforces, and Alyeska Pipeline Service Co. consolidated with layoffs. Anchorage has, for the first time in its history, a service economy. Unfortunately for some of Anchorage's small, locally owned businesses, the explosion of national retailers has brought their end.

City tours include a stop at Earthquake Park for a view of Mount McKinley and Mount Foraker to the north. (Alaskana Photo-Art)

Traditional and modern blend well in downtown Anchorage where the city Christmas tree in Town Square is framed by the Enserch Building. (Harry M. Walker)

It's no wonder the retailers came. Anchorage has long been a center of commerce for Alaska. It's easy to see this in the long lines of people at the always-open main post office who've come in to shop and need to mail home to the Bush what they've bought. Everything from tires to cases of sodas goes out from here, an advantage of low in-state parcel post rates. Retailers are also drawn by Anchorage's relative youth, education and affluence. People here have among the highest household incomes in the nation; the median income for 1995 was $55,700.

A sign of the times: Espresso stands at every turn, selling fancy, flavored coffee drinks at $2, $3 and $4 a cup. It's a Seattle craze come North, in parking lots, in hospital lobbies, in the sports arena, in video and hardware stores. Just as they love to sip espresso, Anchoragites love to gab on their cellular phones, in their car at the intersection, in the back of an airplane, in the aisle of one of those new discount department stores, during a hockey game. Since the technology was introduced here in 1989, 40,000 people have signed up for cellular service.

People here spend lots of money on entertainment. Even on warm, sunny summer evenings, the movie theaters may be as packed as the trails. They splurge on concerts, plays and dinners out, as well as books and music CDs for evenings at home. Grocery markets, particularly home-grown Carrs, rival any big city supermart, with live lobster, sushi, gourmet meats, delis, oriental carryout, bakeries, special candy corners, natural foods sections, liquor stores, and soon to come, smoke shops with imported cigars.

Team sports are big. The city has 88 ballparks and recreation fields, most all of them busy with softball, baseball and soccer in summer. Hockey is so popular that league play goes year-round, with the city's four indoor ice arenas scheduled until late every night and some

mornings as well. During a recent winter, the city groomed the ice on several lakes. Thousands of skaters turned out on Westchester Lagoon on Christmas Day '95, where bonfires burned, a radio station broadcast music and espresso wagons sold hot drinks. Those who didn't skate could buy a wagon ride across the ice behind a team of draft horses.

People here are nuts for outdoor paraphernalia. Nearly 90 percent of the people here own fishing gear and backpacks, and nearly 80 percent of them own tents and bicycles, with hunting gear and skis following close behind. It is often said that the best thing about Anchorage is it's close to Alaska.

Anchorage is a city of commuters: lawyers in Saabs, construction workers in pickups, moms and kids in mini-vans headed to and from school. People routinely drive in from Palmer and Wasilla, an hour north, to work in town. Few residents live close enough to their work to walk from home. A few dedicated cyclists bike everywhere they go, putting on studded or double wide tires for winter riding. The People Mover transit system buses the 6 percent of the city's residents without wheels of their own. The city is dotted with drive-throughs — fast-food joints for dash-board dining, pharmacies, donuts shops and, of course, espresso stands. Some of these are housed in former drive-up banks, victims of the late '80s crash. Anchorage drivers can show surprising courtesy, though. It's not unusual in spring, when migrating water fowl stopover to nest in

Anchorage's roadside wetlands, for drivers to stop and usher a goose and her goslings across a busy intersection.

Anchorage is a city of increasing racial and ethnic diversity with growing numbers of Hispanics, Filipinos, Koreans, Japanese, African Americans, Hawaiians, Samoans, Vietnamese, Thai and Laotian and Alaska Natives. Anchorage has become the biggest Alaska Native village in the state. More than 18,000 Alaska Natives live here, making up 7 percent of the city's population. More Natives live in Anchorage than any other single place in the state; 18.7 percent of all Alaska Natives lived here in 1995. Anchorage also has an increasingly strong link to the Russian Far East with business and cultural exchanges.

FACING PAGE: *Consecrated in October 1994, St. Innocent Orthodox Bicentennial Cathedral serves some of Anchorage's Russian Orthodox community. Archpriest Nicholas V. Molodyko-Harris, who came to Anchorage in 1967, leads the congregation. (Alaskana Photo-Art)*

RIGHT: *A Native from the Nanai region of the Russian Far East performs at the Anchorage Museum of History and Art in one of many cultural exchanges that have taken place between Anchorage and its Russian neighbors. (Harry M. Walker)*

Anchorage's Hispanic community has grown the most of any ethnic group — 49 percent since 1990 and numbered about 13,800 individuals in 1995. The Asian community has undergone a similar increase, as families open groceries and small restaurants to make money to bring other members to town. One of the best Thai restaurants in Anchorage operates from the back of a neighborhood convenience store. For many immigrants, Anchorage is the gateway to a land of opportunity.

As Anchorage has grown, it has acquired big city problems. Poverty and homelessness and crime are on the rise. The city has one of the highest rates of rape in the nation, and drugs, drive-by shootings and gangs take their victims. But it is also a city of compassion, with shelters and food kitchens and churches and a community of caring individuals trying to make a difference.

Although Anchorage has changed in many ways, threads still tie the city to earlier times. Old homes built by the railroad have been restored as lawyers' and doctors' offices along 2nd Avenue downtown. A few of the downtown's earliest buildings still stand, like Kimball's dry goods and Club 25, as well as the art deco 4th Avenue Theater and the KENI Radio building above Westchester Lagoon.

Other traces of old-time Anchorage linger in the personages of early pioneers and landmark namesakes. Fur Rendezvous harkens back to pioneer Anchorage, a feeling evident at the Wild Game Feed hosted each year by Oro Stewart at her photo and rock shop downtown. Continuing

a tradition started 38 years ago by her late husband, she prepares pounds of seal, whale, muktuk, caribou, moose, musk oxen, salmon and pike for her guests to sample. As people pass through the long, narrow store for food, Mrs. Stewart regales them with stories of days gone by, complimenting the most elaborate fur parkas and hats.

BELOW: *Anchorage health enthusiasts can take advantage of this exercise area, part of the coastal trail, along Westchester Lagoon. (Danny Daniels)*

RIGHT: *Anchorage youngsters have done well in national figure skating competitions, spurring other local youths to give figure skating a try. In 1995, Sydne Vogel won the junior ladies competition at the U.S. Figure Skating Championships. In 1996, J.J. Matthews captured the novice ladies national championship. (Alaskana Photo-Art)*

One of the most powerful institutions of old Anchorage remains only as a whisper. In 1989, Bob Atwood sold his *Anchorage Times* to Bill Allen, owner of Veco Corp., an oilfield service firm flush with earnings from oil spill cleanup. Allen closed the paper in 1992, selling all but the land and building to the *Anchorage Daily News*, ending the bitter newspaper war. In one of the most unusual sale agreements ever negotiated in newspaper history, the *Times* retains a presence. The *Voice of the Times*, written by its own staff of three, fills the top half of the *News'* op-ed page. With a pro-development beat, the *Voice of the Times* still echoes an agenda set forth for Anchorage those many years ago, when the first tents went up. ■

Bibliography

Alaska Fisheries Board and Alaska Department of Fisheries. *Annual Report No. 3*. Juneau: Territory of Alaska, 1952.

Anchorage, Crossroads of the World. Anchorage: Anchorage Chamber of Commerce, 1944.

Atwood, Evangeline. *Anchorage, All-American City*. Portland: Binfords & Mort, 1957.

———, *Anchorage, Star of the North*. Tulsa, Okla.: Continental Heritage Press, Inc., 1982.

Browne, Ralph. *Alaska's Largest City, Anchorage*. Juneau: Alaska Development Board, 1953.

Cohen, Kathryn Koutsky. *Independence Mine and the Willow Creek Mining District*. Anchorage: Office of History and Archaeology, State of Alaska, 1982.

Combellick, Rodney, Roger Head & Randall Updike, Eds. *Earthquake Alaska — Are We Prepared?* Report 940218. U.S. Geological Survey with Alaska Division of Geological and Geophysical Surveys and Alaska Dept. of Transportation and Public Facilities, 1994.

Division of Parks and Recreation. *Muldoon Park System*. Anchorage: Greater Anchorage Area Borough, March 1973.

The Economic Base of the Greater Anchorage Area. Anchorage: City Planning Commission, 1956.

Fall, James A. "The Upper Inlet Tanaina" in *Anthropological Papers of the University of Alaska*, Vol. 21, Nos. 1-2. Fairbanks: University of Alaska Press, 1987.

The Great Alaska Earthquake, vols. *Seismology and Geodesy* and *Human Ecology*. Washington, D.C.: National Academy of Sciences, 1972.

Groh, Clifford John and Gregg Erickson. "The Permanent Fund Dividend Program, Alaska's 'Noble Experiment,'" in *The Alaska Journal*, Vol. 13, No. 3. Anchorage: Alaska Northwest Publishing Co., 1983.

Hanrahan, John & Peter Gruenstein. *Lost Frontier, The Marketing of Alaska*. New York: W.W. Norton & Co. Inc., 1977.

Hansen, Wallace R. *Effects of the Earthquake of March 27, 1964 At Anchorage, Alaska*. Geological Survey Professional Paper 542-A. Washington, D.C.: U.S. Department of the Interior, 1965.

Hoagland, Alison K. *Buildings of Alaska*. New York: Oxford University Press, 1993.

Kari, James & James A. Fall, Eds. *Shem Pete's Alaska*. Fairbanks & Anchorage: Alaska Native Language Center, University of Alaska, and CIRI Foundation, 1987.

Nance, John J. *On Shaky Ground*. New York: William Morrow and Co. Inc., 1988.

Naske, Claus-M. and Ludwig J. Rowinski. *Anchorage, A Pictorial History*. Norfolk, Va.: The Donning Co., 1981.

Preuss, Jane. *Configuration of Vulnerability, Reconstruction to the Present Anchorage Bowl, 1964-1994*. Seattle: Urban Regional Research, 1995.

Satterfield, Archie. *The Alaska Airlines Story*. Anchorage: Alaska Northwest Publishing Co., 1981.

Selkregg, Lidia L. *Seismic Hazard Mitigation: Planning and Policy Implementation, The Alaska Case*. Washington D.C.: National Science Foundation, 1984.

Selkregg, Shelia Ann. *Decision and Rational Which Led to Construction on High-Risk Land after the 1964 Earthquake*. Doctoral Dissertation, Portland State University, 1994.

Shannon & Wilson, Inc. *Geotechnical Report Turnagain N.E. Landslide Re-evaluation Anchorage, Alaska*. Municipality of Anchorage, 1989.

Wangness, Paul H. *A History of the Unification of the City of Anchorage and the Greater Anchorage Area Borough*. Anchorage: Anchorage Urban Observatory, 1977.

Wilson, William H. *Railroad in the Clouds: The Alaska Railroad in the Age of Steam, 1914-1945*. Boulder, Co.: Pruett Publishing Co., 1977.

1996 Anchorage Indicators. Anchorage: Municipality of Anchorage, Department of Community Planning and Development, 1996.

Index